Quaker Theology

A Progressive Journal and Forum For Discussion and Study

✥
Issue #26
✥
Winter-Spring 2015

Volume Fourteen, Number One

Editor: Chuck Fager
Associate Editors:
Stephen W. Angell
& Ann K. Riggs

ISSN 1526-7482

All the essays in this issue are copyright © by
the respective authors,
and all rights are reserved by them.

Except where otherwise noted,
the views expressed in articles in *Quaker Theology* are those of the
authors, and not necessarily those of
the Editors, or Quaker Ecumenical Seminars in Theology.

Quaker Theology intends to publish at least twice a year
Subscriptions: US$20 for two issues.
Individual copies/back issues: $10 each, postpaid. From:

PLEASE NOTE NEW POSTAL ADDRESS:

Quaker Theology
Post Office Box 3811
Durham NC 27702

Print copies of this issue can be ordered from:
www.createspace.com

Quaker Theology is also published in an online edition, at:
www.quakertheology.org

ISBN: 978-1508926313

Articles, reviews and letters are welcome.
Authors please send queries first, to the Editor
at the address above.
Or by E-mail at:
qkrtheology@gmail.com

Contents

Editor's Introduction, p. v

Thunder In Carolina: North Carolina Yearly Meeting - FUM
A Report with updates by Chuck Fager, p. 1

Appendix: Letters from Meetings in North Carolina re: NCYM-FUM Controversy, p. 28

Links to NCYM-FUM letters online, p. 72

Quaker theology is not explained by apocalyptic expectation and delay
By Hugh Rock, p. 73

Reviews:

Personality & Place: The Life and Times of Pendle Hill.
Douglas Gwyn.
Reviewed by Chuck Fager, p. 86

Excerpts: *Personality & Place: The Life and Times of Pendle Hill.*
Douglas Gwyn, p. 97

A Convergent Model of Renewal: Remixing the Quaker Tradition in a Participatory Culture. C. Wess Daniels.
Reviewed by Chuck Fager, p. 110

About the Contributors, p. 115

Editor's Introduction

This issue is the longest in *Quaker Theology's* sixteen-year tenure. It wasn't intended to be that. But both weighty events and substantive material kept accumulating, and here we are.

It has also been one of the most arduous issues to prepare. When the disturbances in North Carolina Yearly Meeting-FUM erupted in last summer, we knew there would have to be a report, published as an online Preview; and we uploaded it in late September.

Then the drama extended through November, and into the new year. The impending confrontation on March 7 called for an updated, and more detailed second online Preview. This entailed considerable additional research and was uploaded at the beginning of March. And finally, the arrival of an entirely new yearly meeting – involved in the controversy from its first moment – had to be folded in.

It's not over yet. Will North Carolina's ordeal last for three years, as did the forerunner in Indiana, which we covered here in issues #18-#24? Of course, we don't know that. (We admit it: we hope not.) But we do know we'll do our best to keep up with it, and pass our findings on to you.

❖

Much of the rest of this issue is devoted to a major new work by Douglas Gwyn, writer, thinker, teacher and pastor. He has taken the nearly 90-year history of Pendle Hill, the Quaker study center near Philadelphia, and turned it into an extended and – to me – compelling reflection of American liberal Quaker hsitory in that period.

As acknowledged in the review, your editor, in reviewing Gwyn's book, lacks a certain detachment that one often expects of reviewers. But Pendle Hill's near-pervasive presence in American liberal Quaker life makes such detachment very difficult to find, so we beg your indulgence. (And we recommend you read the excerpts included along with the review, and then the whole absorbing book, and make up your own mind.)

Yet despite our regard for the author, we are not giving Douglas Gwyn a free pass here. Hugh Rock, a British Friend and newcomer to our pages, takes a critical look at Gwyn's apocalyptic interpretation of early Quaker theology, which should be the basis for a lively discussion.

And not least, as press time was nigh, we learned that a manifesto of the much-discussed "Convergent Friends" initiative had appeared, and we hastened to get it, read it, and jot down some thoughts to aid discussion of this latest incarnation of a "new Quakerism."

Despite all the labor, we're confident that you hold in your hands (or see on your screen) a collection of work that is worth the time of thoughtful readers, both Friends and friends of Friends.

– Chuck Fager

Thunder In Carolina:
North Carolina Yearly Meeting - FUM

Chuck Fager

I

As this issue went to press, North Carolina Yearly Meeting-FUM (NCYM) was on the brink of a showdown over its future, with a high probability of undergoing a major schism.

What's at stake in the struggle? Many things, but what stands out are four Ms: Mission, morality, marriage, and money.

The showdown either will – or will not – occur at the Spring meeting of NCYM's Representative Body on March 7. The imminence of a split could take the form of a proposal to "restructure" the yearly meeting (YM), or a walkout by some dissatisfied local meetings. (Two updates follow this report.)

Or the session could deflect and delay a collision, mainly by ignoring the calls for division, or referring them to committees for more study and discussion. And those who see the session as the last stand before bolting could back away from their self-imposed deadlines.

II

To fill in the background of this crisis, one could go back more than a hundred years; but that would turn this report into a book. Suffice to say that over the past several generations, many NCYM meetings have turned into community churches with a what is close to a Southern Baptist culture and outlook.

This church culture, in much of the South, has been for decades a kind of unofficial established church. Southern Baptists are by far the largest denomination in North Carolina, outnumbering the next group, Methodists, by four to one. Given this predominance, the Southern Baptist culture extends far beyond the confines of actual churches. It is accustomed to having its views taken as a baseline, and treated with deference by lesser groups and sects. This church culture is focused above all on what is called "mission," which translates into sending missionaries to convert heathens in distant lands, and building ever-larger church congregations at home. Everything else takes a back seat to this "mission."

However, over the last few decades, the real Southern Baptists, after a long period of growth in membership, have experienced a sharp decline in numbers. Young adults, the so-called "Millennials," have been jumping ship in especially large numbers. And when mission-as-growth is the top priority, decline is not just a setback, it's a sign of religious failure as well.

The exceptions to this downward trend are the so-called megachurches, some of which have grown enormous even while overall church attendance has declined, and many smaller churches are barely on life support. Outside the megachurches, large numbers of Baptist pastors are being obliged to become "bivocational," that is, to take a secular job in addition to church work, because their congregations can't afford to pay them a full-time salary. Other denominations, north as well as south, are reporting similar trends; seminary enrollment is also down.

Two reactions to this trend are common: on the one side, many look to the megachurches as examples to duplicate. And on the other, there is a search for scapegoats: "If it weren't for *[fill in the blank]*, we'd be fine, growing and as vigorous and respected as in the old days." Such heresy hunts and resultant schisms are among the oldest and most enduring of Southern Baptist pastimes.

In NCYM, membership decline over the past thirty-plus years has been dramatic: it has shrunk by more than half, and closed numerous meetings, with no sign of slowing. Along with decline in numbers has come a drop in donation income; drawing up budgets, and then meeting them, has become an increasingly painful and penurious process. The yearly meeting has several million dollars in trust funds, however; and as annual budgets get tighter, these funds look increasingly tempting.

As with the Baptists, both responses to this slide have appeared in NCYM as well. There are no megachurches in NCYM; but a couple could be on the way. The most likely candidate may be Poplar Ridge Friends Meeting in Trinity, which lists a membership of 400, hardly "mega," but large as far as NCYM goes. Further, its pastor, David Mercadante, seems quite sure that his church's path is the model the YM should emulate.

Then there are the scapegoats, for whom "liberals" and "universalists" are the catchall terms of obloquy. This category includes those who question the Bible's ultimate authority, entertain non-traditional notions about Jesus or the Bible, read Universalist Quaker writers such as Philip Gulley, are indifferent to foreign missions, often vote Democrat (even for Democrats named Obama), frequently oppose U.S. wars, affirm LGBT presence in their meetings, could even be LGBT themselves, or – currently the sorest point of all – support same sex marriage.

Countering the Baptist-oriented community church trend, there are a number of NCYM meeting which have gone in this liberal direction. They are a minority, but among them are New Garden Friends in Greensboro, which is nearly as large as Poplar Ridge; First Friends, also in Greensboro; Winston-Salem Meeting; Spring Meeting in the farmland between Greensboro and Chapel Hill; Fancy Gap Friends, a small fellowship just over the Virginia border near Mt. Airy (home of the iconic "Mayberry R.F.D.") and a few others.

None of these "liberal" meetings would look particularly advanced from, say, a northern or western liberal Quaker perspective: all are programmed, most have pastors, and all think highly, if flexibly, of Jesus and Christianity.

But for the Baptist-tinged "mission" advocates, these meetings are more than too liberal; they are a threat. And for NCYM to reverse its decline, the Baptist-oriented conclusion is clear: they must go. Now.

And in the summer of 2014, it was decided, the time had come for their departure. It was overdue, actually.

III

In his pastoral letter of December 2013, Poplar Ridge pastor David Mercadante wrote confidently about war:

> History tells us that a great war requires a great invasion. Before the war can be fought, the offensive force must stage a bold and ambitious attack to breach the opponent's defenses. Everything we know about war tells us that when you invade, you had better be big, bold and powerful.

And so it has been in North Carolina Yearly Meeting (NCYM for short). Beginning in mid-summer 2014, Mercadante was a key figure in organizing a three-pronged assault on what was seen as a corrupt and heretical yearly meeting establishment, in pursuit of what they called "unity" on "core beliefs."

The "offensive" opened with a barrage of aggressive letters, the first of which came from Mercadante's Poplar Ridge Meeting on July 8, 2014. The authors claimed to have identified widespread heresy, "lack of integrity" and dishonesty in officers and members of key YM committees.

The letters demanded the immediate removal of all YM officers and committee members "who will not affirm the basic elements of the Christian faith" as Poplar Ridge and the others interpreted it.

They were especially incensed because several NCYM meetings had "dual affiliation," that is they were affiliated with the Piedmont Friends Fellowship (PFF), a loose association that was organized in the 1960s, and admits meetings of various YMs or none. Besides being alien, PFF's worst sin was its acceptance in the liberal umbrella group Friends General Conference.

"This [FGC connection] creates an obvious and irreconcilable conflict," Poplar Ridge's letter insisted, between its members and "those who no longer affirm our shared confession." All such meetings "should be honest in their assessment and seek other denominational affiliation."

Others spoke out even more forcefully. Two members of Holly Springs Meeting wrote that

> Slowly over the years, liberal thinking groups have infiltrated our Yearly Meeting and now hold some positions on committees. . . . Those who do not believe in the Holy Trinity, those who do not believe in Jesus Christ as our only salvation as the son of God, those who do not believe the Bible as Gods Word, and those who do not believe in our Declaration of Faith set out in our Faith and Practice should be asked to leave the Yearly Meeting immediately and resign all positions held.

Ken Spivey, a longtime pastor, likewise did not mince words: "These meetings should be expelled, ('writen [sic] out of meeting')."

Poplar Ridge also set a deadline:

> Poplar Ridge Friends Meeting has decided that it will not continue to financially support the Yearly Meeting until there is a basic sense of unity among Friends within NCYM. We will meet our financial commitment through March 2015. From that point forward, any monies we would normally pay into Askings will be placed into an escrow account we designate and control. These monies will be released to the Yearly Meeting at such a time as we sense unity and a clear path forward has been achieved. *[NOTE: "Askings" is the term for annual amounts the YM expects each meeting to contribute to the YM budget.]*

Plainfield Meeting's letter set the same date:

> Through much prayer and discernment Plainfield. Friends Meeting has decided that it can no longer support NCYM financially because of severe Theological differences, integrity, stewardship, and the lack of Christ centeredness, among some of our Meetings and among some of the leadership within NCYM. With that being said, Plainfield Friends Meeting will continue to pay 100% of our Askings. to NCYM through March of 2015. Beginning on April 1st

2015, Plainfield Friends Meeting will no longer support NCYM with our Askings. We will withhold all Askings to be paid to the NCYM and we will put them into an escrow account until we feel that NCYM has not only addressed the concerns but **_DEALT_** with these concerns as well. At such a time, when we feel led by the Spirit that NCYM has taken the appropriate measures in the right direction, we will release those funds to NCYM.

[Note Plainfield's five-fold emphasis on "dealt" – bold, capitals, larger type, italics, underlined.]

A dozen such letters, most from meetings, have been collected by *Quaker Theology*; but there may be more. They repeat the talking points set out by Poplar Ridge. Although addressed to the yearly meeting Executive Committee, many circulated widely, and even ended up on the web. (All the ones we have are included in the Appendix.)

This epistolary salvo was soon followed by a "bold and ambitious" siege. It was mounted at the yearly meeting's sessions over Labor Day weekend in September 2014. While the letters came from a relatively small number of the yearly meeting's 72 monthly meetings, carloads of their fired-up members arrived, packed the hall, and were soon making their presence loudly felt.

IV

Two initial targets were the incumbent presiding Clerk, William Eagles, and Jack Ciancio, the Clerk of the YM Executive Committee. Eagles is a member of New Garden Meeting in Greensboro, which was the biggest target of the banish-the-liberals effort.

New Garden is also one of the oldest in the yearly meeting: in 1781 a major battle of the American Revolution was fought around its early meetinghouse; New Garden Quakers tended the wounded and dying of both sides. Now it occupies several acres across the street from Guilford College, founded by Friends in 1837.

But both New Garden and Guilford have long been anathema to the more evangelical elements here. "We should disassociate ourselves," said Ken Spivey, "from any ministry/organization that is not Bible-based and Christ-centered, such as Guilford College . . . ." And on his list of heretical meetings that should be "expelled," New Garden was first.

Eagles' first term as Clerk was set to expire; a second term is usually routine. But opposition was loud and vitriolic, and Eagles quickly announced that he would not seek re-appointment.

That was one down. Next the guns were turned on Jack Ciancio, Clerk of the Executive Committee. Ciancio attends Ararat Meeting, in a small town on the Virginia border, and is a thoughtful sort, no fundamentalist, but hardly a college liberal. Unlike Eagles, he was not up for re-appointment.

No matter. After hours of insult and denunciation, Ciancio left the meeting session and resigned from the committee, reportedly vowing never to serve in a yearly meeting post again.

That was two down. But the challengers wanted more. As it was put by the letter from Holly Springs members

> The Bible is the only authority on scriptural matters. Our Yearly Meeting has become "Unequally Yolked" with individuals and groups who do not share our same belief. . . . Some meetings hold duel memberships in other organizations. Our Faith and Practice prohibits duel memberships. The vast majority of our Yearly Meeting is in total disagreement with these organizations on basic theological issues. . . . A great division has been created in our Yearly Meeting that has caused much strife among us making it impossible to continue. We pray in much distress over this matter but we are convicted that in separation, we can grow once again as a Yearly Meeting.

[Note: spelling is original; and the NCYM Faith and Practice does not in fact prohibit the kind of affiliations represented by Piedmont Friends Fellowship.]

Yet despite all the commotion, the yearly meeting did not separate, and in that respect the assault was blunted. But in response to the uproar, the annual session created a "New Committee", which was charged with examining the concerns and formulating proposals in response, to be presented at the fall meeting of the NCYM Representative Body, on November 1, 2014.

Despite its seeming success, once the annual session dispersed, the third prong of the "big, bold invasion" Mercadante and his colleagues had mounted began to sputter. The road to their vision of "unity" began to seem less clear and straightforward.

V

If there was a roadmap for the campaign, it was outlined by Ron Selleck, a religion professor at Laurel University in High Point NC:

> The time for continued "dialogues" and discussion groups has passed. No administrative tweaking will do the job. Regrettably, the only possible resolution I see is for as amicable a divorce as possible along the lines of Indiana Yearly Meeting. I would spell out the reasons for this conclusion, but I would only be reiterating what the Poplar Ridge letter has already said so well.

The key phrase here is: "as amicable a divorce as possible along the lines of Indiana Yearly Meeting." Selleck also made clear that he has long sought this outcome. Indeed, his advocacy predates his arrival in North Carolina.

In 1991, there was a similar move for forced "unity." It was dubbed "Realignment," and was aimed at Friends United Meeting at large. Had it happened, "Realignment" would have entailed expelling several of the less evangelical FUM-affiliated yearly meetings, and splitting others. Selleck was then the pastor of West Richmond Friends in Richmond, Indiana, and an outspoken champion of "realignment." Indeed, he gave the keynote address at a "Realignment" conference in September of 1991, which was meant to mobilize the "bold and powerful" uprising that would carry the campaign through.

The conference happened, but the "Realignment" didn't. Only one of the FUM yearly meetings (California) formally endorsed the drive; Indiana Yearly Meeting officers, while proclaiming themselves entirely "Christ-centered," were dead-set against separations, and resolutely squashed the effort there. As "Realignment" faltered, California Yearly Meeting left FUM, changed its name to Friends Church Southwest, and joined Evangelical Friends International. Selleck soon resigned his Indiana pastorate, and moved to Carolina.

His views, however, did not shift. And others still in Indiana, who shared his hopes, bided their time, and eventually rose to the top of the yearly meeting ladder. When another opportunity arose, in 2008, they were ready. It came when West Richmond Friends Meeting, Selleck's onetime employer, adopted a "welcoming and affirming" minute, formally opening its fellowship to gays and lesbians.

Readers of *Quaker Theology* will know that we covered what Selleck called the "amicable divorce" in Indiana Yearly Meeting sparked by West Richmond's action over its three year course (see QT Issues #18-#24). We won't repeat those accounts here, except to indicate that they suggest significant differences between Indiana and North Carolina.

For instance, unlike the 1991 "Realignment" struggle, when the yearly meeting clerk was staunchly opposed to a split, in 2008 both the Clerk and the Superintendent were prime movers behind it, and made no secret of their determination. Further, Indiana's Faith & Practice seemed to give the yearly meeting formal authority over monthly meetings, which they were intent on exercising. And in West Richmond they had selected a target group whose members had little stomach for actually pushing back on behalf of preserving its membership in the yearly meeting.

And not least, the Indiana leadership was quite prepared to bend Quaker business practice as far as needed to ensure the outcome they wanted. The retired president of Earlham College, Douglas Bennett, fingered this tactic, both as history and prediction, in a blog post before the crucial business meeting:

> Schisms require some governance fiddle . . . somewhere, somehow in each schism there has been some forcing, some deviation from our best governance practices. We have divided by not finding unity – or declaring 'unity' when there was none."

Bennett then asked, "Will that happen in Indiana?" He soon had his answer.
(Bennet, Doug: "Quaker Fiddle" quote, online at: http://www.quakerquaker.org/profiles/blog/show?id=2360685%3ABlogPost%3A90992&commentId=2360685%3AComment%3A91156)

The evidence for this manipulation was plain to see when the dust settled: their effort to remove a single heretical local meeting was so alienating that in the end eighteen Indiana meetings left. And no Quaker Clerk who can gavel through a decision that overrides the settled opposition of nearly 30 percent of the body's membership is operating by anything resembling honest Friends business process. They got what they wanted, but what the "victors" in Indiana smugly referred to as a "collaborative reconfiguration," was an engineered purge, no more and no less.

And when the "unified" Indiana Yearly meeting gathered in the summer of 2013 for their first purified, slimmed-down sessions, they invited as their keynote speaker – Ron Selleck, to come and take a victory lap, twenty-three years after his earlier setback. No wonder he was ready to see it duplicated in North Carolina.

But as Douglas Bennett might again ask, Will that happen in NCYM?

So far, North Carolina has been different. For instance, the new Clerk, Michael Fulp Sr., the evangelically-inclined Friend who replaced William Eagles, seems doubtful about the idea of a parallel purge, and has showed considerable commitment to Quaker process.

Moreover, unlike in Indiana, the NCYM Faith and Practice contains no provision giving the yearly meeting authority to discipline or expel member meetings, particularly on grounds of heresy. Indeed, although staunchly Christian in outlook, the text states at least three times that it is not to be regarded as a creed.

Then not least, after an initial period of shock, several of the targeted meetings have proved quite capable of standing up for themselves, as we shall see.

For that matter, the condition of some of those demanding "unity" and adherence to the "core beliefs" of the NCYM Faith and Practice present some jarring anomalies.

VI

Consider for instance Poplar Ridge. Its website includes the meeting's own "Statement of Faith," which at the end, notes that it is "adapted from the from the Doctrinal Statement of Northwest Yearly Meeting of Friends." This is intriguing because it is not only imported from another yearly meeting, but from a different branch of Friends.
(http://storage.cloversites.com/poplarridgefriendsmeeting/documents/Statement%20of%20Faith%20-%20PRFM.pdf)

Then consider its worship calendar. As this issue was prepared, the Poplar Ridge website was drenched in a celebration of Lent: "Experience Lent at the Ridge . . .40 Days, 40 Ways"; this was the bold headline on the home page. It also included a bouncy lenten music video.

Which is interesting not only because of the sharp contrast to the traditional Quaker avoidance of "special days", but also because Lent is an invention of the Catholic church, and a key season of the Catholic liturgical calendar. (To be sure, Lent has of late been dipped and scrubbed in a Southern Baptist baptismal font, and the denomination's Lifeway bookstores are packed with Lent-themed "resources." Who would have thought?)

Turn next to Poplar Ridge's adult religious education efforts: for an ongoing women's class, it uses courses and materials by Beth Moore, a Southern Baptist, whose home church excludes women from its ruling body of elders. This too departs from the equal status of women in Quaker ministry. (But then, the Catholic Church and its lenten devotions are also led by an all-male priesthood.) For a mixed class they use work by another popular Southern Baptist pastor and writer, David Platt.

In short, while in the yearly meeting Poplar Ridge sternly denounces outside associations, in its own circle they are chockablock with them: mostly Southern Baptist, but also refurbished Catholic, and a yearly meeting 3000 miles away and from another branch, among others.

In theory a liberal Quaker would shrug at such external explorations: seeking truth wherever it might be found is par for the course.

Yet one wonders if Poplar Ridge could be persuaded that what's fair for them is fair for other meetings; or is it a privilege that comes with the assurance of correct doctrine?

And amid this variety, one strong grey strand is strangely absent: a review of pastor Mercadante's monthly letters, and the meeting newsletter, shows a striking absence of the names of any Quaker worthies beyond the congregation: in reviewing more than a year's worth of material, this reader was unable to find even one mention of George Fox, Margaret Fell, any other prominent early Friend, never mind the pillars of evangelical Quakerism: no Gurney, no Allen Jay, no Lindley Hoag, no Sybil Jones, Levi Coffin, Walter or Emma Malone, or even that spectral presence, the Richmond Declaration.

Likewise absent were references to the broad array of Quaker alphabet groups: no FWCC, EFI, FCNL, FUM, AFSC, USFW, Quaker Volunteer Witness, Right Sharing, the Africa Great Lakes Initiative, et al.

Nor did Carolina Friends bodies fare any better: no mention of Guilford College, or the state's other Quaker schools, Friends Homes, Quaker House, Friends Disaster Service, Mowa, not even the renowned Snow Camp historical drama. The only exceptions were the occasional reference to the yearly meeting

Indeed, in all the available pages of the Poplar Ridge Newsletter, the term "Quaker" seemed to have only two recurring associations: one, with a lake, as many events were held at Quaker Lake Camp; the other is barbecue, which is regularly produced by their "Quaker Men" to raise money for the building fund. (Well, it beats oatmeal.)

Finally, one other feature of most other Quaker groups was also missing from the Poplar Ridge newsletters, what is generally called "Social Concern," and to which NCYM has assigned not one but two committees, Christian Ethics & Morals, and Peace.

To be fair, this area was not entirely overlooked. In his letter of August, 2014, David Mercadante faced one such issue head-on: "What Is The Purpose of Marriage?" was the title.

His answer, which was somewhat disjointed, had to do with becoming holy. He predictably denounced same sex marriage, which then seemed likely to be headed for legalization in Carolina, and concluded that "The national conversation about marriage is one of the most important topics of our day."

It's easy to agree with that last statement. But acknowledging that there were other "important topics" of social concern only highlighted the lack of any of them in his other online letters.

One would, for instance, never know from reading them that the U.S., including North Carolina, was in the grip of a murderous epidemic of gun violence. Or that poverty had increased, or that more black men are in prison today than were enslaved before the Civil War.

Or, speaking of peace, that the U.S. was involved in several wars (with more looming), which have exacted a toll among Carolina troops of almost 1500 killed and wounded just from Iraq and Afghanistan, and many more suffering PTSD and other invisible wounds.

Are none of these, except same sex marriage, worth mentioning in pastoral letters or newsletters at Poplar Ridge?

(Oh, by the way–the reference to battle in the quote from one of Mercadante's letters earlier in this report? That was actually about Christmas. Mercadante was comparing the birth of Jesus to the D-Day invasion of 1944.)

So, has Quakerism been boiled down to barbecue at the lake? One wonders. The nearly total absence of any Quaker content in the recent Poplar Ridge community discourse brings to mind a passage from their initial letter last summer:

> Meetings, just like any organization, are going to shift with each passing generation. No meeting is perfectly static. As a matter of integrity, a meeting should discern if it no longer shares the convictions of her original founding. If a meeting finds itself out of unity with the Faith and Practice which is originally affirmed, they should be honest in their assessment and seek other denominational affiliation.

Who has shifted the most here? An honest assessment, indeed.

VII

The annual session assault soon claimed its first scalp: on September 7, Fancy Gap Friends adopted a minute, which declared:

> It is with a profound sense of sadness that Fancy Gap Friends Meeting has reached the decision to sever our relationship with NCYM. We have seen a fundamental change within North Carolina Yearly Meeting over the past years, as it has chosen a path that we think has turned the body further and further away from Quakerism in thought, conduct, execution of business, and most grievous, in Spirit. We have remained in relationship with NCYM far beyond our ease and comfort, simply in an attempt to be faithful in waiting, to work for the change that we seek, and to bring what portion of Light we might have to our gathered union. Our attempts have repeatedly met with resistance, either in the form of being completely ignored, to outright hostility. . . .

One down, only a handful more to go. Were Poplar Ridge and its allies on a roll?

Maybe. As the autumn advanced, the New Committee, charged with figuring out what to do with the fallout from the annual session outburst, added members from each of the yearly meeting's nine Quarters, sent out a questionnaire to gain a sense of the sentiment in the meetings at large.

So wheels were turning, but on closer inspection the road to an Indiana divorce began to look less direct and perhaps more bumpy than the insurgents had hoped.

For one thing, there were responses to the summer letters from various directions. One particularly eloquent riposte came from High Point Meeting, which has not been among the targeted group. They sent a letter of September 28, 2014, in which they made plain that they were no "liberals":

> We are Orthodox Friends, who love Scripture and claim Jesus Christ as our Lord and Savior, but we cannot unite with the kind of future being claimed by some members of our Yearly Meeting.
> We acknowledge long lasting differences that have led to divisions within our Yearly Meeting. . . .

But then they plainly called out the Poplar Ridge putsch for what it was:

> However, we are disturbed by the judgmental and domineering approach taken by some Friends. While Friends call for theological unity, we fear the strategic aims are to marginalize some members of the Yearly Meeting and form a kind of "unity" through divisions or expulsions. It is our concern that this forceful and divisive approach will threaten vital ministries of our Yearly Meeting, splinter some local meetings, and alienate some members from their meetings. . . .

Further, High Point firmly rejected the notion that either the NCYM Faith & Practice or the Bible, highly as they esteemed both, were meant to be the "ultimate authority" for the body.

> Concerning Faith & Practice: A question the "new committee" is asked to address is "should our Faith and Practice be the ultimate authority in our beliefs and practice and be affirmed by all member meetings?" As we see it, the role of Faith and Practice in a non-creedal society is unique. It is our best effort ("though we see through the glass darkly") to give a sense of who we are and what we believe. It advises Friends on how to function as Christ's community. However, it is not authoritative or final. While it informs our corporate identity and public witness, Friends have often declared that no statements or doctrines can substitute for a personal relationship with Jesus Christ. To require Friends to "affirm" a Faith and Practice as the criteria for membership, in our estimation, makes it creed and the "letter of the law" . . . .

They were even more trenchant regarding the Bible:

We join Friends who hold the Scriptures in high regard, yet we are uncertain by what Friends mean by "Biblical authority." The Bible is subject to human translation, interpretation, and application. For centuries, "Biblical authority" has been used by political leaders to justify wars, slavery, genocide, colonization, and other ungodly enterprise. Most pertinent to our concern for North Carolina Yearly Meeting is the way people use the language of "Biblical authority" to pass judgment and condemnation on others, deny individuals of God-given dignity and grace, silence the voices of women, and implement a spiritual legalism of fear versus love. We also observe that some Christians who insist on "Biblical authority" practice it in selective ways. Many uphold parts of Scripture that support their positions, while ignoring other parts. What do Friends mean by "Biblical authority?" How will Friends determine what is authoritative? Who will make this determination?

Who indeed? And how?

They were almost impatient with the query about outside organizations:

"Why do meetings feel compelled to participate with organizations outside of NCYM?" Quakers are not isolationists. Our ministries are enriched when we participate with other Quaker, ecumenical, service, and mission organizations for numerous reasons.

And instead of setting deadlines, they urged the critics and the yearly meeting to take a more traditional approach:

"Gospel order" is the Biblical inspiration for the Quaker tradition of eldering. The current Faith and Practice urges Friends to follow the "gospel order" when dealing with conflicts between members and meetings . . . . Should this not also apply when dealing with conflicts among Yearly Meeting entities? Have we in North Carolina Yearly Meeting practiced gospel order? How have we sought to reconcile the community?

While calm and traditionalist throughout, the High Point letter was a compelling demolition of the Poplar Ridge case.

And it was not alone.

VIII

Some of the other targeted meetings began to respond on their own behalf. Of these none followed the example of Fancy Gap, which was the smallest of the liberal groups.

The largest, New Garden, seems clear that after 260 years among Friends, it is not going anywhere.

Similarly Spring Meeting, at 240 years and counting, showed no signs of being intimidated.

In its bucolic setting amid dairy farms, Spring did not imagine itself a cutting edge group. Nevertheless, it had reached some clear conclusions in recent years that set it apart from other meetings in its area: for one, a decade ago it had stopped employing a pastor, opting for a programmed, nonpastoral style which it felt was more traditionally Quaker.

And for another, they soon decided they needed to broaden their Quaker contacts, and joined the Piedmont Friends Fellowship.

For a third, as a family-oriented group, the members found themselves drawn to welcome a same sex couple with two children who began attending, as one more family among their number.

And then in 2012, when conservatives in the state pushed for a constitutional amendment to ban same sex marriage in the state (even though it was already illegal), Spring Friends were drawn to oppose it publicly, by placing a small ad in a county newspaper.

Add these together, and the rural white clapboard church was deemed dangerously liberal, even intolerably radical by those determined to obtain "unity" on such matters come what may. The conservative pastor of a nearby meeting attempted to have Spring laid down by its Quarterly Meeting for these "offenses"; but the effort failed.

And Spring Friends were not thrown off balance by the summer assault. Indeed, their response to the demand for the meeting's expulsion, issued two weeks after Fancy Gap's withdrawal, was quite firm, yet unruffled:

> Regardless of the efforts by some to enforce either strict conformity or separation– which only serves to divide, to ostracize, to cast out, our meeting chooses instead to continue to remain a member of this yearly meeting, to seek harmony, not division. We do not consider differences of beliefs among us as threats, but as opportunities for spiritual growth in a world full of God-created diversity. We shall remain. We seek to speak Truth to Power, and to act by the Golden Rule, after the example of Jesus Christ. We do not demand conformity of others, nor do we seek to be bound by expectations of conformity by others. We place little

significance in professions of faith. We ask only to be judged by our actions.

"We shall remain." Thus Spring threw down a gauntlet, yet did so without bluster or bravado: they rejected the purge effort, and set out to resist it simply by continuing to be who they are, and doing what they do.

At the same time, they presented a sharp critique of the rationale behind the Poplar Ridge-led drive, which is worth examining here in some detail:

> We believe that unity is best achieved by embracing of our diversity and, not through the cleavage of our association from others over doctrinal matters. We care not what an individual or congregation claims to profess, placing our highest regard on what they practice. For words, as we have witnessed, often mean little and are callously cast about by some. As George Fox stated, it is not what one professes that is of importance, but what one practices. We shall judge, and ask to be judged ourselves, by the actions of an individual or congregation. It is curious to hear others within our yearly meeting speak of unifying the meeting by use of exclusion and division, by attempting to cast out those with which they perceive do not agree with their absolutist interpretation of Scripture, their world view of social issues of the Day. Within the history of the Society of Friends, as with other faiths, this strategy has repeatedly been applied, only to lead to more division, more misunderstanding, and a distraction away from the true charge of our Faith. That true charge is to demonstrate by our ACTIONS, the love for our fellow persons after the example of Jesus Christ. . . .

They also challenged the idea that a purge would strengthen NCYM:

> We believe that each past schism has weakened our society and inhibited that cause of practicing the example of Jesus Christ. Each current branch of our Society has carried away some strength from the original Society, but has also abandoned some valuable attribute, to its detriment, to another branch. So it will be again if those professing unity through division carry the day. We embrace all branches of the Religious Society of Friends, that diversity begets strength and vitality as we strive to learn from and appreciate one another. . . .

They went on to deconstruct the rhetoric about how the liberal groups were betraying "founding beliefs":

> The "Founding Beliefs" of North Carolina Yearly Meeting: A common theme and quote in many of the recent letters from meetings has been their expectation of adherence to the "founding beliefs" of NCYM. This is a most interesting statement. For the record, North Carolina Yearly Meeting was first organized in the late 17th century, with the first formal gathering deemed a yearly meeting being held in 1697. The Religious Society of Friends and NCYM were founded during that century on the principles that each and every person could have a direct and personal relationship with God, that there was no need for what Fox and other early Friends termed hireling priests, our charge being to "walk cheerfully over the world, answering that of God in everyone". The increased emphasis on Biblical supremacy as compared to the leading of the Holy Spirit was not a founding principle.

And not least, echoing High Point, they not only defended their association with an "outside" group, but affirmed it positively:

> Association with other Friends' organizations: Our meeting is a member of Piedmont Friends Fellowship(PFF) . . . . Our reason for having affiliations with both organizations is to bridge the chasm that unnecessarily exists between these two branches of the Society of Friends, each of which lacks a beneficial aspect of the other. While some members of each organization, particularly within NCYM, seek to widen this chasm and hold no association with the other, we seek a meaningful unity among Friends that such an affiliation can foster.

Articulate, trenchant responses such as Spring's and High Point's to the demand for their departure have gone unanswered, at least in print, by the challengers. But on November 1, as the NCYM Fall Representative Body session assembled, the general response was still clear and unchanged: the Liberals and universalists must go.

IX

The body gathered at Forsyth Friends in Winston-Salem. The meeting room was full, and the purge voices were loud. But they were not unchallenged. And before we get to that, there was other business that came first which deserves mention, dealing with the last of the Four Ms we began with: money.

NCYM is close to being broke, summed up the report. Three staff members had left, and at least two were not being replaced. Programs were being cut back. The pension fund for retired pastors was woefully underfunded. (And the pensions themselves were miserly in any case: a maximum of $450 per month after 30 years service.)

Further, the YM could no longer afford to offer health insurance to pastors. A decade or so ago, in the flush old days, the YM paid for a pastors' health plan; it was a perk. Then the crunch came: costs went steadily up, requirements were raised; and as membership dropped, there was less money to pay the premiums. Many pastors were older, prone to pre-existing conditions and other health issues of age. This also made group coverage harder to find. (Does any of this sound familiar to readers?)

And now, finally, the axe fell: it was announced that the YM could simply no longer afford or find suitable insurance, and was dropping its pastors' health plan entirely.

Yet all was not lost, a committee member assured the group. Rather than being left entirely adrift, pastors formerly on the plan could now seek coverage through "the new arrangements," and many would likely find better coverage there at lower rates.

"The new arrangements?" Irony dripped from this carefully elliptical statement like fat from hot ribs.

For what was being alluded to was the Health-Plan-That-Dare-Not-Speak-Its-Name, the monster that most of those in the room had been told (and believed) for years would spell the end of democracy and the doom of civilization; the program that all successful political candidates in their region swore up and down they would smash and destroy utterly at the very first opportunity.

Yes: These overwhelmingly conservative pastors were now being told to sign up for Obamacare. And to further sour their dispositions, same sex marriage had become legal in North Carolina, by court order, and such weddings had been happening for two weeks.

So when the "New Committee" brought in a set of proposals after lunch, the race was on. There were five, the first dealt with how all meetings could remain in NCYM and produce "effective ministry"; then, whether the Faith & Practice should be the "ultimate authority" in belief and practice, and be affirmed by all meetings; the third asked why some meetings "feel compelled to participate with organizations outside of NCYM"; next, that meetings were expected to support the YM financially; if a meeting didn't pay, its members shouldn't be eligible for YM committees or offices.

Then, the final, bottom line one, #5, asked what might a "restructured or even divided yearly meeting look like?"

All the answers were mostly vague and subject to interpretation, as in fact they had been before: "All meetings should accept the same core spiritual beliefs as set forth" in Faith & Practice; but with no indication of which statements in the book's 150 pages of text embodied this "core."

Likewise, Faith & Practice should be "affirmed" with special reference to the Richmond Declaration of Faith, yet the Committe added that "it should be made clear that affirmation of Faith & Practice does not establish a creed." (Which, we noted earlier, the text itself states three different times.)

Which would seem to say that the ultimate authority states that its text is not to be the ultimate authority. This is a traditional Quaker view, but one unlikely to satisfy the "unity" advocates.

As for participation in outside groups, the committee noted that meetings responded "in a variety of ways." But it also pointed out what had been only recently learned: the Piedmont Friends Fellowship was about to create an adjunct body in the form of a Yearly Meeting, for those of its members which wanted to join one. They were not pleased by this:

> Also, the New Committee is aware that a few of our monthly meetings are considering becoming members of another yearly meeting which represents one of the other major divisions among the Religious Society of Friends. The New Committee recommends that no monthly meeting member of NCYM should become a member of any other major division of the Religious Society of Friends.

As for what a "restructured or even divided yearly meeting" might look like, they punted: merely listed some possibilities, from variations on the status quo to complete dissolution and distribution of all properties and assets and all meetings would "go their separate ways"; with no recommendation for which to choose, if any. They urged committees study the various options.

This was not good enough for the "unity" caucus. There were loud voices saying that one way or another, within a year the YM would be significantly smaller. There was also a fierce personal assault on the character of a woman Friend who had been proposed for the Executive Committee. She had been part of one liberal meeting, the now-departed Fancy Gap, but had transferred to New Garden – jumping from Satan's frying pan into the Anti-Christ's fire.

But there was also pushback. Friends from Winston-Salem, New Garden and Spring all spoke up on their own behalf, generally more irenically than their antagonists. Even so, differences were quite clear. After one of of the hardline pastors declaimed about the critical importance of clinging to Jesus above all, the pastor of one of the targeted meetings, Deborah Seuss of Greensboro First Friends, rose to respond. She was a hundred percent with her colleague regarding devotion to Jesus, she said. "But," she added, "I wonder if you may not want to be in fellowship with me, because I'm willing to marry same sex couples." A good question.

Regarding the item about financial support for the YM, a member of Spring Meeting rose to make a special point: when that meeting decided to drop out of the pastoral system, and revert to a more traditional Quaker worship style, they have calculated that portion of the YM dues which goes to support the pastoral structure, and subtracted it from their contribution. They have also sent in explanations of why they did so. The reduced contribution was not, they insisted, a protest, but a change.

Three other targeted meetings had also been holding back on their expected contributions. Winston-Salem was one, but its member said they didn't have the money: their membership was elderly and declining, and income with it.

New Garden was another, but their motivation was different. Several years ago, they proposed to record a lesbian member as a minister. When they brought this report to their Quarterly Meeting, they were subjected, they say, to torrents of abuse. Their holding back of contributions, wise or not, was indeed a protest against what they saw as unfair and un-christian treatment. But one of their members, Max Carter, told the group that New Garden was reconsidering this action. (The third meeting we will hear from in a moment.)

The chorus of scorn aimed at those who had not paid their full expected amount had a curious aspect: to paraphrase, it was like this: "You're all spawn of Satan, doing the devil's work, abetting the collapse of marriage and civilization, and well along the highway to hell. But before you pass into perdition – don't forget to keep sending us money. In fact, send us some more."

That is a paraphrase, remember, but fair to the way these calls came across. And as a fundraising pitch, one cannot but conclude that *Pay us more so we can keep on demonizing and tormenting you* lacks much persuasive appeal.

This writer has read about people who pay others to beat and abuse them. But what is known of the targeted NCYM meetings strongly suggests that they are not cut from such cloth. At the very least, those making such demands ought to consider whether something more like: *pay up, and we'll at least* pretend *to respect you, the way a server in a restaurant does*, would not go over better.

This concern was stated better by Ken Bradstock, the Clerk of Fancy Gap Friends, in what might be called an "exit interview." Bradstock, who has considerable social work experience, noted that this experience had much to do with why their meeting had withheld its small payments from the yearly meeting. At stake, he stated

> . . . are not only theological standards but behavioral standards as well. It is not so much theology we dispute but behavior.
> Over the last decade, we have seen members and meetings of NCYM (FUM) display cruelty and meanness in their behavior

toward Friends with whom they disagree. We can document those behaviors including a Surry Quarterly meeting wherein our pastor and his wife were harangued for 2 hours with judgments of their character, faithfulness to Christ, and eternal destination to hell. The other incidents will not be described here because we are attempting to keep the tone of this letter positive and healthy. That incident is only meant to be representative of the numerous that we have experienced and have heard about. This kind of behavior feels like a direct violation of the only standard we know of that describes true followers of Jesus Christ.

The only judgment we feel is our place to make is whether this chronic behavior represents a sick institution with harmful behavior. We believe that North Carolina Yearly Meeting of Friends (FUM) is dysfunctional and very much in need of help. We know this by the behavior we observe not through the abstractions of theology. We see cruelty, meanness, manipulation, hostility and codependency. We are not just pointing a finger at those who attack us theologically but those who permit this behavior as well. As most readers know, the family of an alcoholic can be as responsible for the continuation of the disease as the victim himself. We believe that even those in NCYM with whom we align theologically have failed to confront the institution's illness and are complicit as well.

X

By the end of the November Representative Body session, the New Committee's first four vague recommendations were approved. The New Committee was told to bring further guidance about the fifth point on restructuring to the next Representative Body session in March.

But the temporizing on that last item was not for lack of understanding. Rather it set in front of the group the choice that would really move them beyond talk: is the YM really going to expel the targeted group of meetings for heresy? Is there really sufficient resolve to "pull the trigger"?

It is one thing to bluster about a split; it is another to actually force one to occur. If some are ready, how do they plan to get around the lack of authority in Faith & Practice to do it?

Events since November have heightened the stakes, at least rhetorically. Consider:

New Garden Meeting decided in November that it will join the new Piedmont Friends Yearly Meeting – not instead of NCYM, but *in addition to* that affiliation. This is in direct contravention of the New Committee's advice.

At First Friends, pastor Deborah Seuss made good on her statement at the Representative body meeting, and conducted a same sex wedding there in December.

And Spring, as threatened, has carried on as usual, not paying for yearly meeting pastoral expenses; welcoming LGBT attenders and members; and even reading aloud passages from Universalist Quaker author Phil Gulley.

All these are red flags to Poplar Ridge and its allies: *We are still who we are, doing what we do.* What are you going to make of it?

Unspoken, but not far beneath the surface of this interplay is one more dimension of the YM's plight which has been made plain to me since then:

A decision in March, or even later, to expel the targeted meetings, would not be the end of the story. As one well-placed and well-informed Friend stated it to me: "they have been told that if they force a split, the only ones who will benefit will be the lawyers."

And here is another difference between the Indiana scenario and Carolina: Fancy Gap is gone, but the others have made clear that they will not vountarily leave. And without YM authority to force them out, such a coup attempt would be ideal for creating a big payday for lawyers.

Nor is that all. There are several million dollars in NCYM trust funds, to which members from all the meetings have donated. And then there is Quaker Lake Camp. Southeast of Greensboro, Quaker Lake is 104 lovely acres of potential trouble.

The camp is fifty years old, and has roots of labor, money, and family involvement sunk deep throughout the YM. Families from New Garden and First Friends were there at the beginning, donating not only money but time and sweat, and then sending their kids for summer bliss. But not only kids. We noted earlier how often Poplar Ridge holds events there; the same goes for Spring and dozens of other meetings.

Indiana YM had a camp too; but it was less embedded in the hearts of all the meetings. Quaker Lake is different. The idea that the liberal meetings can be forced out, perhaps given a settlement from the trust funds as a sop, then be expected to simply walk away from Quaker Lake, is a pipe dream.

Moreover, unless the YM suddenly were to decide in March to expel the targeted groups and somehow make it stick, whatever outcome does come to pass will take months or years. And then two of the "unity" meetings will face a stark choice: both Poplar Ridge and Plainfield have vowed to withhold their YM contributions beginning in April of this year, unless their kind of "unity" is delivered by then. Other meeetigs have implied as much.

Yet if they do that, then under the rules changes they just demanded and got, their members lose eligibility for YM committees and offices, and their leverage diminishes with that. Cutting off their noses to spite their faces is a phrase that comes to mind.

But if they back off and keep paying – then they've blinked. And that will increase the likelihood that NCYM may simply muddle through, staying together amid the tensions of culture and theology that it encompasses.

Evidently Poplar Ridge, Plainfield and the others would regard this outcome as a great defeat for their hopes of turning the YM structure into a support machine for their kind of evangelism-centered programs. Which is too bad. Because given the strains in American society these days, any group that can manage to stay together while including as broad a spectrum of belief and practice as NCYM is something of a wonder, or maybe even a miracle.

It would also be a prime example of the wisdom of Galatians 6:2: "Bear one another's burdens, and in that fulfill the law of Christ." For is it not the case that these differences are a big piece of the "burden" of religious life in these times?

The standard American response today is to flee it, and take refuge in monocultural enclaves; certainly most nonpastoral liberal Quakers do that.

But is that the correct response? Or is facing and learning to manage such diversity and the tensions it brings more aligned with our actual calling?

High Point Friends' letter may have said it best:

We remind Friends that North Carolina Yearly Meeting and its work belong to God; we are simply His stewards. God is the one who joined this body together, although imperfect and diverse, to reflect His glory and achieve His purposes. The opportunity is now before us to reflect God's power of love and spirit of reconciliation by how we tend to the differences and conflicts among us.

Quaker Theology will follow the course of NCYM-FUM as it grapples with these and related questions in the months to come.

Maybe the road it is on does lead to Indiana.

But then again, maybe not.

❖ ❖ ❖ ❖

Update #1: March 7, 2015.

When the Representative Body again gathered, at Quaker Lake Camp on Saturday March 7, 2015, estimates of attendance ran to 300. There was much oratory and expostulation. Minutes were debated, approved, and deferred. And when the smoke cleared, how much had changed?

Let's see: The New Committee brought in several recommendations (as a handout). Numbers One and Two at first blush sounded draconian:

"1. All meetings shall accept the same core spiritual beliefs as set forth in the NCYM Faith & Practice."

(There followed more than a page of verbiage about God, Jesus, the Bible, and the need for meetings to support the yearly meeting financially.)

"2. Should our Faith & Practice be the ultimare authority in our beliefs and practice, and be affirmed by all member meetings?

"All meetings shall reaffirm NCYM Faith and Practice which includes documents prepared with much care and prayerfuul guidance, such as the Richmond Declaration of Faith, which presents our core spiritual beliefs in a clear, concise manner. Affirmation of Faith & Practice as our guide does not establish a creed."

These two propositions were approved. But as more than one attender was quick to point out later, not was was in them, but what was absent was key. Among the missing features were:

– Any procedure for obtaining the required approvals from meetings: were they to sign something? Write minutes of acceptance? Where and to whom were they to be delivered? What about the meetings which have already stated their principled objections to any such required declaration? Nothing was specified about any of this.

– Any deadline for when such required approvals were to be submitted. When the Spirit moved? Before the Rapture? Next Tuesday?

Plus, if the mandatorily approved Faith & Practice was still not a creed (which codicil, added to those already there, made four such anti-creedal self-descriptions in the Faith & Practice itself), then what did all this posturing amount to?

The answer from several quarters: a lot of hot air, self-contradictory, with no teeth or concrete effect

The purge effort was blunted in another way that afternoon: New Garden Meeting announced that it had decided to pay up its arrerars in yearly meeting dues, so it would no longer be subject to the new restrictions on committee membership in the yearly meeting. This deftly snatched one of the biggest cudgels from the hands of those who had been battering them. It didn't change the theology of the situation; but it could not but affect the politics.

This impression was reinforced when the third item came up:

"3. Why do meetings feel compelled to participate with organizations outside NCYM?

"The New Committee is aware that a few of our monthly meetings are considering becoming members of another yearly meeting which represents one of the other major divisions among the Religious Society of Friends. No Monthly meeting in NCYM shall have dual membership with another yearly meeting. If a meeting feels compelled to join another Yearly Meeting, then they neeed to present their reasons to NCYM Executive Committee and NCYM Ministry and Counsel. (This action will require a change in Faith and Practice.)"

A note on timing: Changes in Faith & Practice can be made only at annual sessions of the Yearly Meeting, which are usually in early September. And any proposed changes must be submitted by two months before the annual sesssion gathers. (F&P, p. 102; 2012 edition).

However, this Proposal #3 was *not* approved by the body on March 7. There were objections, and the Clerk determined that "additional discourse" was neeeded. So the New Committee and others will work on it between March and June, and it, or some revised proposal may be be presented in June.

One other key point: the New Committee was also supposed to make proposals for "restructuring" (i.e., splitting) the Yearly Meeting. But it reported that it had nothing to propose in this regard.

That leaves the issue of dual affiliation. But if some such proposal were approved by the Representative Body on June 6, 2015, it could not be approved by the annual session before September 2015.

The significance of these dates is this: the current Faith & Practice, as noted, does not prohibit such affiliations. And the one meeting which has actually resolved to take on dual affiliation, will have done so many months before. Can such a prohibition be made retroactive *ex post facto*? The U.S. Constitution expressly forbids *ex post facto* laws, with courts having made exceptions in only a few situations, such as that of tracking violent sexual offenders, or perpetrators of domestic violence with deadly weapons. (Article 1, clauses 1 & 3.) This restriction does not cover a church; but the tradition is deeply entwined with public views of fairness. Is Piedmont Friends Fellowship to be equated with violent predatory criminals?

And would it be approved in June? Note again that this was the provision brought forward with an actual concequence – although even here, all that would be required is that the meeting's reasons be "presented" to two yearly meeting committees. Then what?

Whether this proposal will come to anything is yet to be determined. Nevertheless, formally or informally, NCYM-FUM will in fact be obliged to face an actual case of dual membership. Because:

❖ ❖ ❖ ❖

Update #2: March 14, 2015.

Piedmont Friends Yearly Meeting is Born

Piedmont Friends Yearly Meeting opens its first session.

The large meeting room seemed calm enough, but there was a background of controversy for the Piedmont Friends Yearly Meeting (PFYM), which was born the following Saturday, March 14, 2015, after several years of preparatory work.

The woman standing in the photo is Clerk Marian Beane, of Charlotte NC Meeting, calling the first-ever session of the new body to order. The place was the spacious meeting room of New Garden Friends in Greensboro NC, which hosted the gathering.

And there lies the controversy: New Garden, which was not only the host. Its representative soon rose to read a minute of affiliation with PFYM. It thus became the first (and so far only only) formally dual-affiliated Monthly Meeting in North Carolina YM-FUM.

Thus if a prohibition on such connections is enacted in NCYM, there will be only one target: New Garden Friends Meeting.

Several other NCYM-FUM Meetings remain members of the Piedmont Friends Fellowship (PFF), from which the new YM emerged; but they are not joining the new YM itself, which is their option.

This non-YM status may shield them from a prohibition if it is adopted; but they are still targeted by the purge faction on grounds of other purportedly heretical ideas (theological tolerance) and actions (welcoming LGBT folks). But as of March 14, New Garden has quietly thrown down the gauntlet.

The strongest objection to both PFF and the new YM is that they are affiliated with Friends General Conference, the liberal umbrella association. For some in NCYM-FUM, liberal = Satan.

A review of the new body's "Vision Statement & Core Elements" (approved 12/13/14 by PFYM Rep. Body, in handout form) will likely reinforce this impression for many. Here are key "theological" sections:

> SPIRIT– Quakerism began in the 17th century as a Christian movement . . . .While Christian expressions of spirit continue to be central for many Friends, in the 21st century other Friends feel led to describe their experiences in a variety of ways.
>
> Inclusiveness: . . . Rather than prescribing any creed, the Yearly meeting encourages individuals to become part of the corporate experience of Quaker faith and practice. The authenticity of the experience is based on inclusiveness, which in the 21st century, welcomes individuals and families from a wide range of religious traditions and practices and is affirming of diverse genders, ethnicities, racial identification, sexual orientations, ages and beliefs. The Yearly Meeting is composed of monthly meetings with various modes of Quaker worship, understanding that there are multiple legitimate ways to seek and experience the spirit.

So there we have it: LGBT openness, anti-creedalism, and specific de-centering of Christianity within its orbit. Further, the two-page document does not mention the Bible or Jesus, and refers to God only once, indirectly in a quote from George Fox.

The one innovation for a liberal FGC yearly meeting, is that it explicitly permits programmed and pastoral meetings, in light of the North Carolina setting.

This ongoing drama was offstage at the PFYM session, which dealt mainly, as one might expect, with internal organizational matters. But its shadow was there.

Even though NCYM-FUM's next Representative Body session is three months away, there should be some new drama before then: two of the main meetings behind the push for a purge, Poplar Ridge Meeting, and Plainfield Meeting, now confront their own announced deadline that if their version of "unity" was not enacted and enforced in NCYM-FUM by the end of this month (March 2015), both would begin withholding their financial dues to NCYM-FUM. (See their letters, elsewhere in this issue.)

If they make good on this threat, their members will also lose their seats on any YM committees – a rule they pushed for to punish New Garden and other liberal groups. But now New Garden is paid up and eligible.

Will Poplar Ridge, Plainfield and others do it?

And will New Garden be forced to make hard and unwelcome choices? Watch for updates.

APPENDIX:
Letters From Meeting Demanding Disciplinary Action
Against Meetings With Which They Differ –
And Responses

[Note: The letters are reproduced here, and are also online at our website. Links are listed after the letters. **The quality of reproduction is as good as we could make it from the available copies.**]

Bethesda Friends Meeting, Dunn, North Carolina

Dear NCYM Executive Committee, Staff, Ministry & Counsel, and Monthly Meetings:

Bethesda Friends Meeting would like to respond to the letter from Poplar Ridge Friends Meeting dated July 8th, 2014. "If a house is divided against itself, that house cannot stand." (Mark 3:25) We have a sincere concern for the current state of NCYM and all the meetings that are affiliated with the Yearly Meeting. It is our firm belief that the Yearly Meeting should be unified in its foundational belief in Jesus Christ and the authority of scripture.

Bethesda Friends Meeting is a Christ centered meeting that believes that there is only one salvation that is offered which is only through the sacrificial work of Christ Jesus who lived a sinless life, died on the cross for our sins and was raised to new life by God the Father for our justification. We believe that God will only give grace and righteousness to those who trust in Christ alone as their Savior who is the mediator for us between God and man.

We would like to note that Items 1, 2, 3 & 4 in the letter from Poplar Ridge are of great concern to us and realize that they cannot be overlooked or "pushed to the side" and need to be addressed by all meetings that make up NCYM. We as a meeting will be in constant prayer that the foundation that our Yearly Meeting was built on (The Faith and Practice which is based from the teachings of God's written word the Bible) does not waiver or change but stands through generations today and into the future. Hebrews 13:8 says "Jesus Christ is the same yesterday, today and forever."

At this time Bethesda Friends Meeting will continue to support NCYM financially and pay our Askings but fully expect all meetings to acknowledge that we can only continue to be Disciples of Christ if we are unified so we can move forward. We request that these items be addressed by NCYM, all Monthly Meetings in NCYM and all committees of NCYM and feel the March 2015 time that is mentioned in the letter from Poplar Ridge is a reasonable time frame to have a direction.

We will continue to pray and ask the Holy Spirit for wisdom and direction to see us through this time.

Read and approved by Bethesda Friends Meeting on Ministry and Counsel – August 7th, 2014.
Read and approved by Bethesda Friends Called Monthly Meeting – August 17th, 2014

Don Lee, Ministry & Counsel Clerk

David Carroll, Monthly Meeting Clerk

Deep Creek Friends Meeting, Yadkinville NC

To: NCYM Executive Committee, NCYM Clerk, NCYM Superintendants, each Meeting within NCYM

From: Deep Creek Monthly Meeting

Re: Concerns relating to the Listening Sessions, Organizational Assessment Survey and letter from Poplar Ridge Meeting

Dear Friends,

Our stated vision at Deep Creek is that we strive to be *A COMMUNITY OF FRIENDS growing in God's Word, reaching all generations, and serving others in Christ's love.*

We are concerned about the winds of discord blowing through our Yearly Meeting. These winds have given us cause to consider what we believe and although we found the impetus for these considerations to be of great concern, the process has encouraged us to be thoughtful and deliberate in discussions of our faith. George Fox, in his letter to the Governor of Barbados, sums it up pretty well. We believe in God and in Jesus Christ and believe that He was made a sacrifice for sin, who knew no sin, that He was crucified, buried and rose again, that He ascended and now sits at the right hand of God to intercede with God the Father on our behalf. We do believe that the Holy Scriptures were given by the Holy Spirit of God, that they are to be read, believed and fulfilled and that He that fulfills them is Jesus Christ. (paraphrased from Extract from George Fox's letter to the Governor of Barbados) We hold that any seeking that identifies "Light" from any source other than God the Father, Jesus Christ His Son and the Holy Spirit is false and not worthy of consideration by members of NCYM. (paraphrased from 1 John 2:22-25 and the Richmond Declaration of Faith)

We assert that what we do as Friends should be considered with a three-part test. Is Jesus Christ at the center? Is this rooted in Biblical faith? Is this committed to and rooted in the Quaker expression?

If we are true to ourselves, and have any integrity at all, we will review our beliefs as members of this organization. If any of us as members, and possibly as member Meetings, upon such evaluation, see that we no longer are in accord with the "General Doctrinal Statements" as set forth in *Faith and Practice*, then we should consider following the lead of the Wilbur-Gurney separation, and more recently NCYM-Conservative, and seek affiliation with those more closely aligned with our beliefs. We need to go where we are fed.

Deep Creek Friends Meeting - Page 2

For many years theological differences have inhibited us from operating with the level of trust and accord that is vital to our mission and purpose. We have allowed confusion about the basic tenants of our faith to go unanswered, thus creating an atmosphere of uncertainty and mistrust among us. There have been valiant efforts to reconcile our differences over recent decades which have not met our needs. As painful as separation would be; is another split a viable option for us? How can we move forward?

There are tangible parts of NCYM that are shared by all, *i.e.* QLC, Pastor's retirement funds, MOWA, NC FDS, *etc.* There will be delicate and complex issues relating to a separation. However, the greatest act of care and love for one another could be to release those with differing beliefs to the path they feel led to follow.

Structure of the Yearly Meeting administration, staffing considerations and financial affairs of the Yearly Meeting are all important but remain secondary to the clear statement and requirement that our core beliefs center on Jesus Christ. In order to be a member of NCYM, participate and have a voice in its ongoing business, individuals and Meetings must affirm the core beliefs of NCYM as stated in *Faith and Practice*.

Until we can agree on Jesus, we can never have hope of "Claiming the future God has for us."

Read and approved at Deep Creek Monthly Meeting in session 8th Month, 10th Day, 2014

Walter Shore, Clerk of Monthly Meeting

Roger Holt, Clerk of Ministry and Counsel

FORBUSH FRIENDS MEETING

August 6, 2014

To: North Carolina Yearly Meeting, Executive Committee, Staff, and Monthly Meetings

Forbush Friends is writing this letter to communicate our deep concerns with the distorted spiritual direction of several meetings and some of their members. The Yearly Meeting is now suffering from a lack of unity which has led to conflicts in ministry, staffing, and committees because of disagreement on fundamental truths of our Christian faith. The result is a Yearly Meeting that is too busy with conflict to build God's Kingdom or fulfill our primary function which should be leading people to a saving relationship with Jesus Christ.

Our key concerns are focused on three issues:

1. Disagreement on the Person and Work of Jesus Christ

- It is a fundamental truth that Jesus Christ is the Son of God and more than just a good man, a teacher, or a "light." *"but these are written so that you may believe that Jesus is the Christ, the Son of God, and that by believing you may have life in his name."* John 20:31

- It is a fundamental truth that a personal faith in Jesus Christ as our Savior brings salvation from our sins which reconciles us to God. *"But if we walk in the light, as he is in the light, we have fellowship with one another, and the blood of Jesus his Son cleanses us from all sin."* 1 John 1:7

- It is a fundamental truth that Jesus Christ is the only way to our Heavenly Father. *"Jesus said to him, 'I am the way, and the truth, and the life. No one comes to the Father except through me."* John 14:6

2. Disagreement on the Authority of the Bible

- It is a fundamental truth that the Bible is the inspired Word of God. *"All Scripture is breathed out by God and profitable for teaching, for reproof, for correction, and for training in righteousness,"* 2 Timothy 3:16

- It is a fundamental truth that any continuing revelation that disagrees with the Bible is not from God. *"Beloved, although I was very eager to write to you about our common salvation, I found it necessary to write appealing to you to contend for the faith that was once for all delivered to the saints. For certain people have crept in unnoticed who long ago were designated for this condemnation, ungodly people, who pervert the grace of our God into sensuality and deny our only Master and Lord, Jesus Christ."* Jude 1:3, 4 There is further, this bold statement in our Faith and Practice(pg. 130), "...and whatsoever anyone says or does, contrary to the Scriptures, though under professions of the immediate guidance of the Holy Spirit, must be reckoned and accounted a mere delusion."

- It is a fundamental truth that we must guard against people who abandon Christ for a distorted belief in something else. *"I am astonished that you are so quickly deserting him who called you in the grace of Christ and are turning to a different gospel—not that there is another one, but there are some who trouble you and want to distort the gospel of Christ."* Galatians 1:6-7

3. Disagreement on integrity in membership of NCYM

- We believe it is a lack of integrity that leads Meetings to withhold askings with no formal reason given so discernment and restoration can be attempted.

4460 Forbush Road, East Bend NC 27018   336-961-2519   www.forbushfriends.org

Forbush Friends Meeting, Page 2

- We believe it is a lack of integrity that leads Meetings to financially support other religious organizations and Yearly Meetings while they refuse the same support to NCYM.
- We believe it is a lack of integrity that leads members of Meetings to keep positions on committees, boards, or as clerks where they can influence decisions without fully supporting NCYM.

While Forbush's initial response is to submit this approved letter of concerns, we will continue praying for peace and unity for our body of believers through a return to the fundamental Christian beliefs upon which NCYM was founded. As a Meeting, we are considering other options if steps are not taken soon to correct the spiritual course of North Carolina Yearly Meeting.

Read and approved by Forbush Friends Meeting on Ministry and Counsel

_____ Date 8/6/14

Charlie Crews Jr, Ministry and Counsel Clerk

Read and approved by Forbush Friends Monthly Meeting

_____ Date 8/6/14

Leroy Hobson, Monthly Meeting Clerk

4460 Forbush Road, East Bend NC 27018   336-961-2519   www.forbushfriends.org

HOPEWELL FRIENDS MEETING

August 3, 2014

Dear NCYM Executive Committee, Stewardship/Finance Committee, Staff, and Monthly Meetings,

Hopewell Friends Monthly Meeting met on August 3, 2014 and considered a letter addressed to quarterly meeting clerks from the NCYM stewardship/finance committee soliciting feedback about the current askings formula, and an organizational assessment survey conducted by the NCYM executive committee soliciting feedback about the organizational and leadership models of the yearly meeting. Even though one was addressed to quarterly meeting clerks and the other to individuals, Hopewell Friends felt the need to address both of these as we express our concerns as a meeting.

Hopewell Friends Meeting is more aware than ever that there are significant problems that need to be addressed within North Carolina Yearly Meeting. Perhaps the most apparent indication of these problems is our financial dilemma which seems to be getting worse. We see three major components to our current financial dilemma: 1) a significant loss of membership in the last few decades; 2) a significant and lingering downturn in the economy; 3) a significant lack of unity within our Yearly Meeting in regards to elements of both our faith and our practice that has resulted in specific meetings not paying their askings as a protest. While we as a yearly meeting ought to be addressing all three components, Hopewell's current concentration is on the third.

Our frustration at Hopewell is multi-faceted. First, we are frustrated with the decision made by local meetings not to pay their askings. Secondly, we are frustrated that the yearly meeting has not been more assertive in responding to these meetings about their unpaid askings. These problems have existed for many years and are not getting better. In fact, they seem to be quickly getting worse.

We have several recommendations in handling our financial issues that may help us to better handle their underlying causes.

1. Meetings that do not pay their full askings should detail, in writing, their reason(s) for not doing so. If a meeting is financially unable to pay, they should state so. If a meeting is not paying all or a portion of their askings as a protest, they should state their reason or reasons for such an action. This should be sent to local meetings. Hopewell has had to pay more in askings every year because there are some who refuse to pay. We should know exactly why they have chosen to make us pay more than our share to cover the costs they are unwilling to cover. We feel this is a simple act of integrity.

2. Any meeting that is not paying all or a portion of their askings as a protest should detail, in writing, all of the changes they deem necessary to bring them back to a position where they would pay all of their askings. For example, would they want committees to act differently, do they see significant

2244 Hopewell Friends Rd. • Asheboro, NC 27205 • (336) 629-0641
2 Corinthians 5:17-20

Hopewell Friends Meeting - page 2

policy changes, are they asking for changes to *Faith and Practice*, which sections of *Faith and Practice* would they change, etc.

3. Any meeting that is not paying all or a portion of their askings as a protest should lose some benefits of the membership in NCYM that they are not paying for. The first of these should be that they will not have any of their members serve on yearly meeting committees of any kind or as officers. This should result in immediate resignations from their members that are currently serving in those roles. Other benefits that are lost might be their ability to use Quaker Lake at discounted prices. Protesting meetings might not be able to sign up until after other meetings have had the chance, and they might be asked to pay full market value for the facilities they use. While we are cautious not to make pastors suffer for the decisions of their meeting, if they don't support those decisions, we feel that pastors who are in protest of the yearly meeting might voluntarily turn down their benefits, such as health insurance, as an act of integrity.

4. We feel strongly that meetings should not hold duel affiliations, especially when they might support the mission of one group financially while not fully supporting NCYM financially.

Our hope is that as we address the issues most specifically related to our current financial dilemma, we can do so in a matter that will enable us to more fully deal with its underlying cause that we would identify as our lack of unity. It becomes increasingly obvious that many within North Carolina Yearly Meeting do not share common ideals. Many are increasingly willing to disregard essential tenets of the Christian Faith, including the atonement of Jesus Christ, and are increasingly willing to disregard the authority of Scripture. We believe that it is as a result of these diversions from unity that some of the members of NCYM are withholding their askings because their views are not being accepted and affirmed by the rest of the yearly meeting. They are refusing to pay their fair share of denominational expenses and forcing others to pay more than their share at the expense of the ministry of our own local meeting.

These four issues of unity are the most important that we have to deal with:

1. Being in unity about the person and work of Jesus Christ, the only begotten Son of God and the Savior sent to save us from our sin.

   Even though the *Faith and Practice* of our yearly meeting has clear statements about the Lordship of Jesus Christ, and includes an extract from George Fox's Letter to the Governor of Barbados and the Richmond Declaration of Faith which speak to those beliefs, and has recently reaffirmed those statements of faith, they are not being lived out by some in our midst.

2. Being in unity about the authority of the Bible.

   Again, even though the *Faith and Practice* of our yearly meeting has clear statements about the ultimate worth and authority of the Bible, and includes an extract from George Fox's Letter to the Governor of Barbados and the Richmond Declaration of Faith which speak to those beliefs, and has recently reaffirmed those statements of faith, they are not being lived out by some in our midst.

While some might argue that Quakers are non-creedal and should not have to have agreement on belief statements, Quakers in our yearly meeting still feel the need to "make some declaration of the fundamentals of our faith." (*Faith and Practice*, 2004, p. 27) It is very obvious that everyone has beliefs, even those who claim they are non-creedal. The question is not whether we have beliefs but whether they are clearly defined and whether we are in unity about them. The truth of the matter is that at some point all meetings affirmed our Faith and Practice. If some do not still hold to that affirmation, they should realize that they have moved.

Hopewell Friends Meeting Letter - Page 3

3. Proper sharing of financial responsibilities.

   In order for there to be any integrity and equality among our community of meetings, all meetings must pay their fair share of our shared financial responsibilities if they are able. Not paying those askings places unfair and undue strain on other meetings and seems to be a lazy way to engage in profitable discussion about issues we disagree on.

4. Integrity in our committee structures.

   In order for our committees, especially our executive committee, to operate with the trust and integrity they need, we feel that they should take specific steps to avoid any appearance of impropriety. Therefore, we feel that: 1) No person should ever serve on the nominating committees of both the yearly meeting and ministry and counsel at the same time. 2) No person on nominating committee should ever be nominated to fill a position on a committee under the purview of that nominating committee, especially to the executive committee. If this has happened, it should be rectified immediately. 3) No person who is a representative in any way to another yearly meeting should serve on the executive committee of our yearly meeting. Once again, if this has happened, it should be rectified immediately. Because any appearance of impropriety could greatly damage the credibility that the executive committee has with local meetings, we believe that any and all occasions of impropriety should be brought to the light and handled in the light. 4) Again, no person who is a member of a meeting not fully paying their askings should serve on any yearly meeting committee, with the exception of those who are financially unable. If this has happened, it should be rectified immediately.

As a result of these problems in NCYM, Hopewell Friends is prayerfully considering our support of NCYM. Please hear us clearly, we still want to be a part of the yearly meeting and want to fully support it financially. However, we urgently want for the yearly meeting to be unified in its foundational beliefs in the person and work of Jesus Christ and the authority of the Bible. We also want the yearly meeting to be unified in its commitment to financial and structural integrity.

To that end, we sincerely ask for the leadership of our yearly meeting to quickly institute a process whereby the yearly meeting might address the issues and concerns brought forward by our letter and others like it. We feel that time is of the essence and that the yearly meeting can no longer afford to avoid this conversation.

Hopewell Friends feels the need to make it known that if quick progress is not being made, the yearly meeting should not budget for 2015 expecting to receive our full financial support. We have currently made no decision to withdraw our support and we don't intend for this statement to be taken as an ultimatum. However, we do not want the yearly meeting to plan for 2015 counting on funds that may not be there.

Hopewell Friends Meeting is excited about the possibility of a unified yearly meeting and we hope to contribute positively to a process where that might be achieved. We are also praying for our yearly meeting, its leadership and its future role in spreading the gospel of Jesus Christ!

Sincerely,

Brian Hunt,
Clerk, Monthly Meeting

Myra Brady
Clerk, Ministry & Counsel

Daniel Thames
Pastor

PINE HILL FRIENDS MEETING
3968 NC HWY 268
ARARAT, NC 27007
336.374.4396

August 13, 2014

To the Attention of North Carolina Yearly Meeting, Executive Committee, North Carolina Yearly Meeting Ministry and Counsel, Committees, Staff and Monthly Meetings:

Pine Hill Friends Meeting writes to you acknowledging the concerns identified by a letter recently received from Poplar Ridge Friends Meeting. We would like to thank Poplar Ridge for leading the effort to bring these concerns to light. After review of Poplar Ridge's letter, Pine Hill Friends supports the stance Poplar Ridge has taken and recognizes the same concerns as critical to the future of our Yearly Meeting. Pine Hill has a long standing relationship with supporting the Yearly Meeting both spiritually and financially. Through our relationship with the North Carolina Yearly Meeting, Pine Hill has been able to achieve more toward building the Kingdom of God and sharing the message of Jesus Christ. It is through this past success that we see unlimited potential of a united Yearly Meeting.

We would like to outline and share with you what we feel are the barriers that are limiting the ability for our Yearly Meeting to grow and realize God's full blessings. Those barriers are as follows, but not limited to;

1. A basic fundamental disagreement over the authority of the Holy Scripture and the person and work of Jesus Christ.

We believe that Jesus Christ was born of a virgin, lived a sinless life on earth while fully man and fully God. He was crucified and died on a cross for our sins. Jesus Christ was placed in a tomb following his death but arose on the third day from the tomb. He is presently at home in Heaven and at the right hand of God interceding for you and me each day. He is the truth, the life, and the only way to God. You must believe that Jesus is the son of God and that he died on a cross for you and arose from the dead in order to receive Salvation and eternal life in Heaven. Furthermore, we believe that the Bible is

1

Pine Hill Friends Meeting Letter - Page 2

God's holy word and final authority given to us and inspired by the Holy Spirit. Pine Hill Friends affirms and recognizes God's Holy Word as the final authority.

Jesus said, "I am the way, the truth, and the life. No one comes to the Father except through me." John 14:6

2. **A refusal by member meetings within North Carolina Yearly Meeting to recognize the NCYM Faith & Practice as our book of discipline and operating principle.**

Understanding that no theological writing takes the place of God's holy word, we believe the NCYM Faith & Practice and Richmond Declaration of Faith provide basic understanding and direction on how we as Meetings and individuals should conduct ourselves. Pine Hill Friends affirms these writings and realize their importance in the ability for our Yearly Meeting to operate successfully. We feel confident that the practices NCYM has expressed in our book of discipline are clear in defining integrity. We feel that Meetings who do not align themselves with our book of discipline should seek other avenues of affiliation.

3. **The refusal of member Meetings to pay Askings out of protest.**

While we realize some Meetings cannot pay their Askings due to financial hardships, there are other Meetings that refuse to pay their Askings out of protest to NCYM positions on social issues and concerns. Pine Hill Friends has long believed we can do more for the building of God's Kingdom and have far greater outreach by working through a larger body of believers who are Christ centered. The refusal to pay Askings has placed hardship across NCYM for Meetings in good standing to absorb the shortfall in revenue. It is our hope that one day we will have a Yearly Meeting where all Meetings can and will meet their financial obligations.

4. **NCYM Leadership positions being held by Members of Meetings that do not pay Askings or recognize the NCYM Faith & Practice Book of Discipline.**

Pine Hill Friends feels that anyone serving in a Yearly Meeting level leadership role should be a Member of a Meeting that is in good standing both spiritually and financially with the NCYM and its doctrine. The refusal for someone in a leadership role at Yearly Meeting level to affirm the NCYM Faith & Practice brings to light concerns

Pine Hill Friends Meeting Letter - Page 3

regarding integrity. We feel anyone who does not affirm the basic guidelines of our faith should not be afforded the opportunity to serve in any capacity at the Yearly Meeting.

Pine Hill Friends celebrates 115 years of loyal service to our Lord and Savior Jesus Christ, to the Pine Hill community and to the North Carolina Yearly Meeting. Pine Hill Friends has seen a lot of changes through those 115 years. We have grown from thirty-one dedicated charter members meeting in a brush arbor in 1899 to 154 members in 2014, meeting in the comfort of modern buildings. One thing that has not changed during that time is our dedication for seeking God's will through discernment and prayer. It is through that discernment and prayer that we have faith that God is in control and will guide us through these concerns. We value the North Carolina Yearly Meeting and the work of those before us. We know there are aspects of the Yearly Meeting that are working well and those include Quaker Lake, MOWA, Friends Disaster Service, Friends Campus Ministry, USFW, NC Quaker Men, as well as Kenya and Jamaica mission fields. As we go forward Pine Hill Friends will stay aware to the happenings within North Carolina Yearly Meeting and take any necessary steps to secure the spiritual and financial condition of our Meeting. Pine Hill Friends has no plans to leave the North Carolina Yearly Meeting or withhold our Askings. We do anticipate a resolution to our concerns that are both Biblical and that will rebuild integrity across our North Carolina Yearly Meeting. We look forward to working with you in creating a North Carolina Yearly Meeting that is in unison to bring others to know Christ.

Read and Approved by Pine Hill Friends Meeting on Ministry & Counsel
-August 13, 2014

Tadd Noonkester, Ministry & Counsel Clerk

Approved by Pine Hill Friends Monthly Meeting
-August 10, 2014

Bob Ring, Monthly Meeting Clerk

3

Plainfield Friends Meeting
1956 Plainfield Church Rd., Siler City, NC 27344

Pastor, Kevin Rollins
Ministry & Counsel Clerk, Sandra Cooper
Monthly Meeting Clerk, Gwen Headen

August 10, 2014

Dear North Carolina Yearly Meeting Executive Committee, Ministry & Counsel, and Monthly Meetings:

Plainfield Friends Meeting is writing to you with a strong sense of urgency and discernment about the ongoing disunity among some of the participating Meetings in NCYM. We at Plainfield feel that there are issues within NCYM that need to be addressed and dealt with. In the letter from Poplar Ridge, they have outlined some of our same concerns and we do not wish to re-state those here. We wish only to affirm what our stance is and will be as we push forward into the future with our affiliation with NCYM.

We would like to voice our concern over the ongoing issues that continue to plague the NCYM at almost every level. There are several concerns, which in our discernment, are heretical and have not been dealt with as they should be. We will not list the concerns here for Poplar Ridge has addressed most of them already. Most Meetings within NCYM know what these concerns are and have known for quite some time now. It greatly concerns us that the leadership in NCYM does not deal with these concerns but rather sweeps them under the rug in hopes that they will go away. These concerns have gone un-dealt with for long enough and NCYM as a whole is reaping what it has sown.

Through much prayer and discernment Plainfield Friends Meeting has decided that it can no longer support NCYM financially because of severe **Theological differences, integrity, stewardship, and the lack of Christ centeredness**, among some of our Meetings and among some of the leadership within NCYM. With that being said, Plainfield Friends Meeting will continue to pay 100% of our Askings to NCYM through March of 2015. Beginning on April 1st 2015, Plainfield Friends

Meeting will no longer support NCYM with our Askings. We will withhold all Askings to be paid to the NCYM and we will put them into an escrow account until we feel that NCYM has not only addressed the concerns but **DEALT** with these concerns as well. At such a time, when we feel led by the Spirit that NCYM has taken the appropriate measures in the right direction, we will release those funds to NCYM.

Plainfield Friends Meeting will continue to support the many ongoing missions and ministry programs that NCYM has in place with our finances, our time, and with our prayers. These programs include MOWA, Friends Disaster, Belize school, Jamaica, Quaker Men, USFW, Quaker Lake, FCM, etc. We feel like these programs reach and minister to many people in and out of NCYM. All of these ministries are extremely important and we will support them in any way that we can.

This decision was not easy, for we feel that NCYM could be a beacon of light to a lost world and could be beneficial for all of North Carolina and not just to Friends Meetings. We feel that this Yearly Meeting has an opportunity to reach untold numbers of lost and misguided souls throughout the world and everywhere in between if we can get back to focusing on the person and work of Jesus Christ. We sincerely pray that these concerns will not be taken lightly as in the past but dealt with honestly, with the utmost integrity, and with much discernment through the conviction of the Holy Spirit.

Approved by Ministry & Counsel August 10, 2014
Approved by Monthly Meeting August 10, 2014

Sandra P. Roper

Gwen H. Hesler

Kevin Rollins

Poplar Ridge Friends Meeting

3673 Hoover Hill Road | Trinity, NC 27370
Office: 336.861.5026 | prfriends.org |
poplarridge@prfriends.org

David R. Mercadante, Senior Pastor
Brian Donley, Associate Pastor
Mark Allen, Monthly Meeting Clerk

July 8, 2014

Dear North Carolina Yearly Meeting Executive Committee, Staff, Ministry & Counsel, and Monthly Meetings:

Poplar Ridge Friends Meeting is writing out of a deep sense of spiritual conviction over our participation within the North Carolina Yearly Meeting of Friends. As outlined below, we have a series of pressing concerns that have burdened our hearts for a long time. We believe that our Yearly Meeting can be unified, can enjoy God's blessings, and can grow in number and influence. However, we believe that we cannot move forward as a Yearly Meeting until the source of our division is addressed.

Through much prayer and discussion, we name the following issues to be the most troubling:

1) **A crucial disagreement about the Person and Work of Jesus Christ and the Authority of Scripture.** We believe in Jesus as the sole, exclusive atonement for sin as written in the Holy Scriptures. He is not equal with other gods, but superior and unique. We believe the scriptures are true in claiming that Jesus is the only way to the Father (words from our Savior Himself) and without Him we fall under condemnation. It is increasingly clear that all Friends do not share our convictions about Jesus Christ. This is not something we believe has occurred in one single event, but that it has grown in gravity and voice over the past three decades. We welcome diversity of belief and understand that there are several Christological appropriations, but we also realize that powerful ministry cannot happen without a basic agreement of the Person and Work of Jesus Christ.

2) **A lack of integrity among member meetings of NC Yearly Meeting who no longer affirm the NCYM Faith and Practice.** While no theological writing fully expresses the entire scope of the Living God (nor attempts to), we realize that documents such as the Faith and Practice and the Richmond Declaration have a tremendous power to unify and empower Friends to minister on a broad scale. Meetings, just like any organization, are going to shift with each passing generation. No meeting is perfectly static. As a matter of integrity, a meeting should discern if it no longer shares the convictions of her original founding. If a meeting finds itself out of unity with the Faith and Practice which is originally affirmed, they should be honest in their assessment and seek other denominational affiliation. Further, some meetings enjoy a dual-affiliation with NCYM and other Quaker Organizations that do not share the core tenets of our faith (specifically Friends General Conference and Piedmont Friends Fellowship - soon to become its own Yearly Meeting in March 2015, see: piedmontfriendsfellowship.org/pff-member-meetings/). The bulk of NC Yearly Meeting continues to proudly affirm the NCYM Faith and Practice while some of its meetings follow an entirely different Faith and Practice that is in alignment with beliefs of Friends General Conference. This creates

Poplar Ridge Friends Meeting - Trinity NC - Page 2

an obvious and irreconcilable conflict with those who no longer affirm our shared confession. No substantial ministry can flow from such division. The mere fact that some meetings have dually affiliated with other organizations confirms our belief that these meetings have <u>drifted</u> from the founding beliefs of NCYM (Faith and Practice) while the majority of NCYM still holds to the original founding tenets of our organization.

3) **Meetings that refuse to pay Askings out of protest.** Our Yearly Meeting does not have a problem with the way we collect or calculate Askings. Our problems are much deeper than budgets. There are some meetings that cannot pay their Askings due to financial constraints and/or decreasing attendance and we certainly sympathize with those meetings. However, it is unacceptable that some meetings (specifically New Garden, Winston-Salem and possibly more) have not been paying and continue to withhold their Askings. Although no specific reasons have been publicly stated for these refusals to support the entire expenses of NCYM, it is presumed to be out of an ongoing protest to the convictions of the larger body. We do know that some of these protesting meetings have been specifically supporting certain programs (Friends Disaster Service, MOWA, Quaker Lake), but have chosen to not support the organization in general. The result of this long remonstration has been an increased financial burden on the meetings that do meet their obligation. This has also led to an inability to adequately staff positions within our Yearly Meeting office, a growing divide between liberal and evangelical meetings and a constant tension that hinders worship, fellowship and outreach among the wider Body of Friends. This has placed an extra burden on meetings that faithfully pay their Askings and created a relentless cloud of discord hanging over the Yearly Meeting. Furthermore, it has been impossible to truly discuss these important issues because these meetings have either neglected or refused to communicate why they are not paying.

4) **Some Yearly Meeting leadership (clerks and committee members) come from meetings that do not affirm NC Yearly Meeting Faith and Practice.** How can any organization thrive (or even survive!) while the leadership disagrees with the core convictions and principles of their own organization? As a matter of integrity and fairness, Friends who affirm the Faith and Practice should be the only ones who are able to serve in leadership. We feel that any member of our Yearly Meeting who will not affirm the basic elements of the Christian faith as outlined by Faith and Practice should not serve on committees or in leadership.

Our concerns are not just limited to these theological, financial and administrative elements. Our greatest concern is that it is impossible to do substantial, God-ordained ministry together. We are proud of the projects that all meetings can do together, regardless of theological leanings. Friends Disaster Service is a good example of project coordination for a common good. However, we believe our ministry together should be *more than projects*; it should be about discipleship under Jesus Christ. If we believe drastically different things about the gospel (i.e. the nature of humanity, the atonement of Jesus, necessity of salvation in Christ, etc...) then our aim of discipleship will not be the same. We simply cannot be in unity regarding our desire for our membership and for the world. How can we make disciples together as a Yearly Meeting if we have such differing beliefs? How can we plant churches? How can we have integrity in our recording process? Our main responsibility is to make disciples and we cannot do that if we endure fundamental disagreements on the One to whom we seek to emulate,

Poplar Ridge Friends Meeting - Trinity NC - Page 3

worship and serve. We are wise to heed our Lord's counsel, *"If a house is divided against itself, that house cannot stand."* (Mark 3:25).

<u>Therefore, with great caution and much discernment, Poplar Ridge Friends Meeting has decided that it will not continue to financially support the Yearly Meeting until there is a basic sense of unity among Friends within NCYM.</u> We will meet our financial commitment through March 2015. From that point forward, any monies we would normally pay into Askings will be placed into an escrow account we designate and control. These monies will be released to the Yearly Meeting at such a time as we sense unity and a clear path forward has been achieved.

We realize the audacity and irony of our refusal to pay Askings partly because we are not in unity with meetings that do not pay Askings. However, this step is necessary because:

- *We will continue to support the Yearly Meeting once there is unity. We have not seen evidence that those meetings who are currently protesting NCYM by withholding their Askings have any plans to express their concerns or to return to financial integrity.*

- *We are clearly communicating our convictions in hopes of an ongoing period of discernment and subsequent action. There have been plenty of strongly worded letters written over the years, evaluations, vision groups, and a plethora of minutes that have been approved; none of which has brought resolution to our core issues. Unfortunately, we feel that our concerns are not going to be heard or addressed unless this step is taken. Hopefully, attaching our concerns to our Askings will spur a serious and more urgent conversation.*

We hope that local meetings, the Yearly Meeting Body, Executive Committee, Ministry & Counsel and any governing bodies in our Yearly Meeting will take meaningful steps towards creating unity. Again, we are eager to pay our Askings to a Body that has a clear and meaningful mission. Until then, we cannot continue to support a Yearly Meeting wrought with division.

At Poplar Ridge, we are excited about the possibility of a unified Yearly Meeting. We desire for the entire world to know Jesus Christ as Savior and enjoy discipleship under our Great Shepherd. We have the best intentions for NC Yearly Meeting and hope that our action is understood and addressed.

Read and approved by Poplar Ridge Meeting on Ministry & Counsel - July 1, 2014.

Bobby Beane
Bobby Beane, Ministry & Counsel Clerk

Read and approved by Poplar Ridge Friends Monthly Meeting - July 8, 2014.

J. Mark Allen
Mark Allen, Monthly Meeting Clerk

Email from Ron Selleck, Professor of Religion,
Laurel University, High Point NC

(Email from Ron Selleck dated July 17, 2014:)

Dear Jack Ciancio,

I have received your Email on behalf of the Executive Committee. I cannot express myself any better than the recent letter recently sent out by Poplar Ridge Friends. We have had a perpetual show of hands for the twenty years I have been part of NCYM, yet through it all a determined tail has managed to wag the dog. The Poplar Ridge letter is exactly right in describing our disorder that those who are least responsible to the Faith and Practice of NCYM and most financially irresponsible create among us at the very core. The time for continued "dialogues" and discussion groups has passed. No administrative tweaking will do the job. Regrettably, the only possible resolution I see is for as amicable a divorce as possible along the lines of Indiana Yearly Meeting. I would spell out the reasons for this conclusion, but I would only be reiterating what the Poplar Ridge letter has already said so well.

Either NCYM is a part of Christ's Church or it is simply a religious social club. The proof will out. It has been too much the latter for too long. As things stand now, I am troubled that my recording as a minister of the gospel has become meaningless, NCYM's witness having become so diluted by our modern day Ranterism. I do not want to be welcome where Christ's supposed friends are ashamed of the cross and choke at the gospel and treat the scriptures as a loose leaf notebook to make their own additions and deletions.

Ronald Selleck, PhD
Professor

To the Listening Session:
From Southview Church, Business Mtg, Aug 3.2014

Dear NCYM

The great hope for North Carolina Yearly Meeting lies in the super group of Young Adults and Young Friends currently involved in our denomination. However, if we do not correct a core problem, we will lose most of these great "kids" to other parts of the Kingdom of God that are not so dysfunctional. In fact, we have been made aware of some who have already given up on Quakerism, and/or left faith entirely after witnessing the behavior of adults at NCYM.

Southview has been, and remains, extremely loyal to NCYM and the general doctrine of Friends. We have sacrificed to pay Askings. We believe NCYM offers opportunities to do things that we cannot do as individual meetings, such as Mexico Mission, Intern programming, Campus Ministry, etc. We believe our theology and doctrine to be superior to all other groups because we believe the Quaker way is the closest of all to the New Testament. But, the structure of our Yearly Meeting is severely flawed. One of our members says that in 40+ years of attending NCYM business meetings, he can never remember attending a single business meeting that had unity of Spirit when anything of significance was discussed. The Ministry & Counsel meeting at Forsyth in 2011 was not an aberration; it was a clear example of typical, usual, Quaker procedure.

Someone at that meeting used the word dysfunctional. We ARE dysfunctional. Not as defined in that meeting, but in the sense that we can't function at all. The only types of business we accomplish is routine, nonessential, and only on limited projects, such as Disaster Service, can the 2 sides of NCYM work together.

We are divided. There are two distinct groups in the Yearly Meeting and we may as well admit it and stop pretending that we have "unity but diversity." We do NOT have unity-we have two different core beliefs. One group is referred to as "evangelicals"; the other group identified themselves at Forsyth as "universalists." But that still does not identify the problem sufficiently: the evangelicals say that universalists cannot be Christians according to the evangelical definition of both words. The universalists claim to be Christians by their own definitions of the two words. Indeed, tempers flared at Forsyth over this very conflict of "Christian or not." The core problem is that evangelicals want their theology determined by a book, while the other side believes theology should be determined by inner self. Neither side will budge from their core. Persons on opposite sides of a chasm can talk all they want about unity, but they cannot hold hands. Bridges cannot be built when neither side trusts the other.

Jesus said a house divided cannot stand (Mk 3:25). Oil and water do not mix. Hugh Spaulding described this Yearly Meeting as a covered wagon with a horse on each end pulling in opposite directions. This Yearly Meeting needs to recognize and admit our core division, and for the mutual benefit of both sides, stop fighting and simply divide. It is ironic that those who have proclaimed the message of peace, do not have peace among ourselves and never will so long as this persists. Let's go separate ways so there can be peace.

There is an story about a lion and a lamb that lived in the same cage at a zoo. Visitors were always amazed that the lion and lamb could co-exist in the same cage. One day a visitor asked what the secret was for coexistence. The zookeeper answered- 'I put a new lamb in the cage every night." We are eating each other up- Let's get different cages.

We would rather present to the coming generation a smaller, but structurally sound Yearly Meeting, than the odd, dysfunctional, mess that now exists. Believing this, we want to affirm the letter written by Poplar Ridge dated July 8, 2014. NCYM must find a way to either bring unity according to our Faith and Practice, or to separate and create new functioning bodies. To continue talking is fruitless- it has all been talked over many years without meaningful change. Also, simply ignoring the problem fixes nothing.

Unless this division is solved, there is no point in talking about Superintendents, Staff, Vision, Direction, Purpose, etc. Solve the issue now so the work of the Kingdom may go forward.

We have been asked to give solutions. The only solution we can see is for the two sides to agree to go separate ways.

Regrettably, but sincerely, approved by Southview Church

Chris Blamer, Clerk
Mike Wall, Pastor

Letter from Ken Spivey

August 9, 2014

Ken Spivey
1547 Cox Brothers Rd.
Asheboro, N.C. 27205

N.C.Y.M. Executive Committee

Committee Members,

  As per your request concerning input concerning the future of North Carolina Yearly Meeting, after having served six years on the Executive Committee, I that I must remind the current members that their's is to **make** recommendations to the Representative Body for that body's action, not to **set** policy.
  Now, about this idea of the Yearly Meeting being the final authority, **Never!** Any Bible believing Christian (Christian being one who believes in the diety of Christ) knows that the Holy Bible is the final authority. This is my stand. And, if I understand the Faith and Practice correctly, this is Friends' belief as well. I quote from the 1981 edition, 1999 printing, page 128:
  It has ever been, and still is, the belief of the Society of Friends that the Holy Scriptures of the Old and New Testament were given by inspiration of God, that, therefore, there can be no appeal from them to any other (outward) authority whatsoever, ...
  If we are going to survive as a Yearly Meeting, our Yearly Meeting **must** be composed of like-minded meetings. **Never** must we become a hodge-podge of meetings wherein each meeting can believe whatever they want and still belong to North Carolina Yearly Meeting of Friends.
  The apostle Paul is recognized as the greatest missionary ever. What made him so great? Was it his good looks, his persona, exactly what? It was his

belief in Christ Jesus as his Savior and Lord and his devotion to this same Christ Jesus. And, Christ cannot be one's Lord unless He is first and foremost one's Savior. Again, if North Carolina Yearly Meeting is going to survive, we **must** stand firmly upon the diety and atonement of Christ, the inspiration and authority of the Holy Bible, what sin is and how to get salvation, as well as the Biblical teaching that marriage is the union of **one** man to **one** woman.

Because some of our meetings have strayed from these teachings, we have become unequally yoked together with unbelievers. I am in total agreement with items 1 - 4 addressed in the letter from Poplar Ridge Friends Meeting, dated July 8, 2014.

Now we come to our theological issues/differences. In order to be a life changing, vibrant Church, we **must** be in unity/agreement concerning the basic/ essential truths of the Christian faith, **and** we should support **only** those ministries that are Bible based, Christ-centered ministries. We should disassociate ourselves from **any** ministry/organization that isn't Bible based and Christ-centered, such as Guilford College, Ramalah Friends School, F.C.N.L., and others. This disassociation should include those meetings who have chosen to join, or support, other organizations/yearly meetings, such as Friends General Conference and Piedmont Friends Fellowship. These meetings should be expelled, ("writen out of meeting"). This includes meetings as New Garden, Winston Salem, Spring, and any others who hold a different view of Christ and the Holy Scriptures that most meetings in North Carolina Yearly Meeting hold. I believe that such double-mindedness makes it impossible for us to continue to attempt to work together. I also believe that anyone adhering to teachings contrary to the Holy Scriptures should not be allowed to hold **any** position of responsibility within the Yearly Meeting. Those holding such positions should resign immediately.

"But you're being unkind and unloving." Not so. Was Christ being unloving when He called the Jewish leaders to account? Was Christ being unloving when He cleansed the Temple? Absolutely not! What was doing was trying to get these people to see the error of their ways. And that is what I hope to accomplish here, to help these misguided people see the error of their ways. Because that is what the love of Christ is about, to bring these people to repentance and belief in Him as Savior and Lord.

What is really unkind and unloving is for these people to blaspheme the name of Christ Jesus after what He did for them at Calvary and through that empty tomb. Hear! Hear!

The sad fact is, we are a "House divided," and a house divided cannot stand. I believe that the only way North Carolina Yearly Meeting can ever move forward is for the above mentioned meetings, and others like them, to leave the Yearly Meeting.

What can be done to insure Christ-centered, Bible based doctrine within North Carolina Yearly Meeting? What are some solutions? For one, I believe we need an addendum to the Faith and Practice. We need a provision for the Yearly Meeting to be able to better enforce theological issues. If a meeting should stray from Christ-centered, Bible based Doctrine, the Yearly Meeting should be able to discipline them, and, if need be, remove them from membership.

The same is true for the recording of ministers. The N.C.Y.M. Recording Committee, along with the Yearly Meeting Ministry and Counsel should have the authority to reject anyone if they do not adhere to sound Biblical doctrine as laid out in Faith and Practice.

Most Friends believe the biblical concept of marriage. That marriage was instituted by God for the purpose of procreation, and that it is to be between **one** man and **one** woman. If procreation is the purpose of marriage, will somebody please tell me which partner in a homosexual marriage will have a baby. You know, God is pretty smart after all, isn't He? The Holy Scriptures are very adamant that these so-called homosexual marriages are in direct violation of God's will and plan for mankind.

What are some needs of North Carolina Yearly Meeting? To begin with, we need to be a unified body of believers who preach and teach the same things, like the diety of Christ Jesus, the infalability and authority of the Holy Bible. Our chief goal should, no, **must be,** to win the lost to Christ, then disciple them in the faith that they too can go out and win others.

As quickly as possible, with much prayer and supplication, we need hire a Christ-centered, Bible believing superintendent with some level of authority for guidance, even discipline in regards to ignoring sound Biblical doctrine.

The same pertains to a Director of Youth and Intern Ministries. This individual must be a Christ-centered, Bible believing individual who can, and will, lead and teach our youth in the ways of Christ Jesus.
We must continue to support and expand Friends Campus Ministries as a means of reaching and discipling college students for Christ Jesus.
Thank you for your attention to these matters.
In the Love of Christ Jesus,

Ken Spivey

Copy to: Hugh Spaulding
          Brent McKinny

Yorks - Holly Springs Meeting

North Carolina Yearly Meeting of Friends

Executive Committee/Stewardship Committee/Finance Committee

We have chosen to respond to your email of July 17, 2014 in the form of this letter instead of the NCYM Organizational Assessment Survey. This survey bothered us greatly as it did not disclose who this survey came from. If it came from the executive committee, we fear you have greatly overstepped your authority and failed to address the real problems of our Yearly Meeting. We would like to address these questions.

(1) The Bible is the only authority on scriptural matters. Our Yearly Meeting has become "Unequally Yolked" with individuals and groups who do not share our same belief. Slowly over the years, liberal thinking groups have infiltrated our Yearly Meeting and now hold some positions on committees. Some meetings hold duel memberships in other organizations. Our Faith and Practice prohibits duel memberships. The vast majority of our Yearly Meeting is in total disagreement with these organizations on basic theological issues. Those who do not believe in the Holy Trinity, those who do not believe in Jesus Christ as our only salvation as the son of God, those who do not believe the Bible as Gods Word, and those who do not believe in our Declaration of Faith set out in our Faith and Practice should be asked to leave the Yearly Meeting immediately and resign all positions held. A great division has been created in our Yearly Meeting that has caused much strife among us making it impossible to continue. We pray in much distress over this matter but we are convicted that in separation, we can grow once again as a Yearly Meeting.

(2) In the Matter of Asking's. Some meetings have stopped paying their asking's in protest of issues.
    We believe that any Meeting not paying asking's should not benefit through insurance for pastors as other Meetings who faithfully pay. It is impossible to meet our financial obligations each year in the Yearly Meeting budget and even pay staff members. All members should pay the same.

(3) Missions. We are glad to support Christ centered mission projects at home and in other countries, however we need to be more focused on leading souls to Jesus Christ. This is our great commission to go into the world. Organizations such as FCNL, AFSC, Guilford College, Ramallah Friends School and others do little to speak to this great need. A lot of financial support has gone to these organizations over the years with little regard to the real mission work in the world.

It is with much prayer and deep spiritual conviction that we address these issues and concerns that have divided our Yearly Meeting for years. We feel that the full ministry of Quakers has greatly suffered from this division. <u>We insist</u> that these concerns be addressed at our upcoming Yearly Meeting Sessions and swift action be taken to finally be a Yearly Meeting of unity.

      Elvin and Linda York,

      [signature]

      Members of Holly Spring Friends, Southern Quarter

Responses:

Fancy Gap Friends Fellowship

High Point Friends Meeting

Spring Friends Meeting

Fancy Gap Friends, Fancy Gap, Virginia

Step One:

From Fancy Gap Friends Fellowship

Friends:

It is with a profound sense of sadness that Fancy Gap Friends Meeting has reached the decision to sever our relationship with NCYM. We have seen a fundamental change within North Carolina Yearly Meeting over the past years, as it has chosen a path that we think has turned the body further and further away from Quakerism in thought, conduct, execution of business, and most grievous, in Spirit. We have remained in relationship with NCYM far beyond our ease and comfort, simply in an attempt to be faithful in waiting, to work for the change that we seek, and to bring what portion of Light we might have to our gathered union. Our attempts have repeatedly met with resistance, either in the form of being completely ignored, to outright hostility.

With this notice we officially withdraw from the body that has for so long filled our business agendas, burdened our hearts, and sapped our energies. Though we regret the necessity of leaving the body of NCYM, we are hope-filled that this act will enable us to return more fully to the work that we are called to do. Way has opened for us to enter a Yearly Meeting of Friends who seek the Spirit in its multiplicity of forms, who are dedicated to Quaker process, and who are not offended by our presence among them.

Though we leave NCYM with disappointment, we leave with clear minds and a sense of hope that, on a different path, we might help create a Yearly Meeting community of unity, joy, and peace once again. Friends, we also wish this for you.

Approved Ninth Month 7th Day, 2014

Signed by the members & associates

Fancy Gap: Additional Comments,
By Clerk Ken Bradstock:

Friends:

The letters sent out regarding division in North Carolina Yearly Meeting of Friends (FUM) seem to beg a response. Fancy Gap Friends Meeting has decided that it should express its concerns as well.

We believe that the doctrines stated by (list meetings) are acceptable and established through many years of work and conviction for many Christians. We also believe that the meetings who made clear their adherence to those doctrines are sincere and strongly believe what they stated. We as a Friends Meeting respect their right to state those beliefs and practice them to the best of their ability.

Fancy Gap Friends Meeting also understands that the meetings that wrote the letters were expressing a form of Christianity known as "Fundamentalism" that is often used pejoratively to express the 5 fundamentals of Christian belief as formulated by theologians at Princeton University and the Niagara Bible Conference around turn of the 20th century. We know that it was, and continues to be a response to Modernism and higher criticism of the Bible. We want it understood that we are not using the term "Fundamentalism" pejoratively but as a way to describe the system of belief expressed by the above-mentioned meetings.

With that said, we wish to express our concerns that have arisen out of that system of theology for us.

Fancy Gap Friends Meeting does not believe that a list of 5 fundamental doctrines describes anybody as a Christian. We cannot find those doctrines stated by Jesus as tests for true believers. The only statement we can find is Jesus simple statement that his followers can be identified by their fruits (Matthew 7:20). That statement alone is risky for us to use because Fundamentalists will point out that some of our standards are evil thus proving ourselves to be out of line with scripture. However, when we begin looking for the definition of good fruit, we find that Paul stated clearly in Galatians that the fruits of the Spirit are "love, joy, peace, patience, gentleness, and meekness. Herein, as we believe they, are not only theological standards but behavioral standards as well. It is not so much theology we dispute but behavior.

Over the last decade, we have seen members and meetings of NCYM (FUM) display cruelty and meanness in their behavior toward Friends with whom they disagree. We can document those behaviors including a Surry Quarterly meeting wherein our pastor and his wife were harangued for 2 hours with judgments of their character, faithfulness to Christ, and eternal destination to hell. The other incidents will not be described here because we are attempting to keep the tone of this letter positive and healthy. That incident is only meant to be representative of the numerous that we have experienced and have heard about. This kind of behavior feels like a direct violation of the only standard we know of that describes true followers of Jesus Christ.

The only judgment we feel is our place to make is whether this chronic behavior represents a sick institution with harmful behavior. We believe that North Carolina Yearly Meeting of Friends (FUM) is dysfunctional and very much in need of help. We know this by the behavior we observe not through the abstractions of theology. We see cruelty, meanness, manipulation, hostility and codependency. We are not just pointing a finger at those who attack us theologically but those who permit this behavior as well. As most readers know, the family of an alcoholic can be as responsible for the continuation of the disease as the victim himself. We believe that even those in NCYM with whom we align theologically have failed to confront the institution's illness and are complicit as well. We apologize if this seems harsh but we believe we must speak truth to power and Fancy Gap is certainly small in numbers. In the current state of NCYM, being a numerical and theological minority is a disadvantage. One of the behaviors we observe is the trend toward a democratic model in business which bows to majority rule.

Our decision to withhold askings is not what we see in other meetings. We are not attempting to punish yearly meeting. Our askings are too small to even consider that motive. We did, however wish to bring these problems to light. In the dysfunction of NCYM, we believed that one way to do that is to call attention to the behavioral problems. Also, we do not believe that it is healthy to focus primarily on money or membership as NCYM's indicator of strength. We strongly believe that the indicators are: love, joy peace, longsuffering, gentleness and meekness. Paul points out that there is no law against those things and we agree with his assessment. NCYM still holds some level of those fruits but they seem to be growing weak and falling off of the tree as they atrophy under the pressure to become Fundamentalist and democratic in theology and business procedure.

We believe that it is time for NCYM to let go of futile and endless debates about theology and Quaker procedure and look at behavior. We also believe that our theological and procedurally kindred meetings join us in addressing the dysfunction in YM directly and with strength.

Step Two:
Fancy Gap Friends Meeting, Fancy Gap VA

New Beginnings

Posted on January 27th, 2015

Here at Fancy Gap, our meeting has a new name. We are no longer Fancy Gap Friends Fellowship, but are now officially Fancy Gap Monthly Meeting of the Religious [Society] of Friends. And we also have a new affiliation. After many years in North Carolina Yearly Meeting FUM and Friends United Meeting, last summer we left both and are now a part of Piedmont Friends Fellowship and Yearly Meeting, and a member meeting of Friends General Conference.

This was not an easy decision and it was made with a great deal of pain and regret. But their were two issues that we were simply unable to accept as being in keeping with Quakerism as we understand it. One has to do with our belief in the total equality of all people before God which has led us to be a welcoming and affirming fellowship. Because of that stance , this was not a hypothetical issue. Members of our meeting who we love and cherish were hurt time and time again by the cruel things said to them and about them. We finally reached the point of saying, enough is enough and determined not to subject these Friends to any more of the kind of treatment they had received in the past.

The other is our understanding that from the very beginning Quakers rejected any attempt to have a creed or any series of doctrinal propositions imposed upon them. There are many Friends in our former Yearly Meeting who were quite vocal in their demand that all meetings be subject to the Richmond Declaration and the Yearly Meeting Faith and Practice.

It was very clear to us that whether or not Friends agreed with these documents, no meeting or individual should be forced to accept or adhere to them in order to be a part of a Yearly Meeting. It became increasingly clear to us that this was the direction in which the Yearly

Meeting was moving, and since we appeared to be the ones out of step with that, it was time for us to leave.

We have found the last six months to be a time of refreshing and of joy. Our meeting and its ministries to the community are continuing to flourish, largely because our time and energies are now focused on making God?s presence visible to those around us and doing very positive things in the world rather than allowing the negativity of some Quakers to prevent us from doing the work at hand

- See more at:
http://fancygapfriendsfellowship.com/#sthash.RXE8kxSM.dpuf

High Point Friends

September 29, 2014

Fellow Friends of North Carolina Yearly Meeting,

800 Quaker Lane
High Point, NC 27262
www.highpointfriends.org
Phone: 336-884-1359

    Representatives from High Point Friends Meeting came away from the 317th Annual Session of North Carolina Yearly Meeting saddened and alarmed. The subtitle for these sessions was: "Claiming the Future God Has for Us." We are Orthodox Friends, who love Scripture and claim Jesus Christ as our Lord and Savior, but we cannot unite with the kind of future being claimed by some members of our Yearly Meeting.
    We acknowledge long lasting differences that have led to divisions within our Yearly Meeting. We respect deeply held convictions expressed by Friends in letters and addresses to the Yearly Meeting body. We appreciate the civil approach of Friends as they communicated these concerns. However, we are disturbed by the judgmental and domineering approach taken by some Friends. While Friends call for theological unity, we fear the strategic aims are to marginalize some members of the Yearly Meeting and form a kind of "unity" through divisions or expulsions. It is our concern that this forceful and divisive approach will threaten vital ministries of our Yearly Meeting, splinter some local meetings, and alienate some members from their meetings.
    As we read the letters and listened to our representatives' reports we are led to share these concerns and ask these questions:
    Concerning the Person and Work of Jesus Christ: We join Friends in the desire for a unified witness of the person and work of Jesus Christ. We caution Friends to guard against: hardening of one's heart, making statements in anger, conveying of harmful rumors, and demanding Yearly Meeting reforms based on

perceptions and unverified truths. Friends, what do we gain if we attain a unified Christology but lose Christ-like love, gentleness and forbearance? We are confused by non-specific assertions that the Yearly Meeting or its members are denying Jesus Christ. Yearly Meeting sponsored programs, camping activities, mission endeavors, and publicity are clearly Jesus Christ- centered. No proposals have come to the Yearly Meeting body to change or challenge historic faith statements about Christ.

From the floor of the Yearly Meeting body, our representatives heard notions that some Friends focus on Christ's work of atonement and evangelism while other Friends focus on Christ's work for justice and peace. Are these aspects of Christ's ministry incompatible? Are not both needed for a unified witness of the person and work of Jesus Christ?

Concerning Faith & Practice: A question the "new committee" is asked to address is "should our Faith and Practice be the ultimate authority in our beliefs and practice and be affirmed by all member meetings?" As we see it, the role of Faith and Practice in a non-creedal society is unique. It is our best effort ("though we see through the glass darkly") to give a sense of who we are and what we believe. It advises Friends on how to function as Christ's community. However, it is not authoritative or final. While it informs our corporate identity and public witness, Friends have often declared that no statements or doctrines can substitute for a personal relationship with Jesus Christ. To require Friends to "affirm" a Faith and Practice as the criteria for membership, in our estimation, makes it creed and the "letter of the law." What happens to Friends who cannot "affirm" or do not follow certain aspects of the document (i.e. statements on alcohol consumption, tobacco use, joining secret societies, gambling, baptism, or peace)? Will they and their meetings be barred from membership and leadership in the yearly meeting?

We urge Friends to reflect on the advice given to early Friends, found in the opening paragraphs of our Faith and Practice: Dearly beloved friends,these things we do not lay on you as rule or form to walk by, but that all with the measure of light which is pure and holy may be guided, and so in the light walking and abiding these may be fulfilled in the spirit, not from letter; for the letter killeth, but the spirit giveth life. (Faith & Practice: North Carolina Yearly Meeting of Friends, page 10) We believe this advice is the proper application of Faith and Practice.

Indeed, it is good for Friends or Meetings to examine themselves in the "measure of light" and determine if they are abiding in the "spirit" of Faith and Practice. If Friends or Meetings persistently live outside the "spirit" of Faith and Practice or become obstructionists to those who strive to do so, it is incumbent upon concerned members of the Yearly Meeting to caringly exercise "gospel order" (Matthew 18:15-17). We are advised to make an attempt to reconcile Friends to the community before other extreme actions are taken. "Gospel order" is the Biblical inspiration for the Quaker tradition of eldering. The current Faith and Practice urges Friends to follow the "gospel order" when dealing with conflicts between members and meetings (Faith & Practice: North Carolina Yearly Meeting of Friends, page 84). Should this not also apply when dealing with conflicts among Yearly Meeting entities? Have we in North Carolina Yearly Meeting practiced gospel order? How have we sought to reconcile the community?

Concerning Biblical Authority - Again, we are Friends who love the Bible. It is the written Word of God which contains the story of salvation, the gospels of Christ, which offers devotional hope and prophetic guidance. Robert Barclay writes that the Scriptures are "a full and ample account of all the chief principles of the doctrine of Christ" (Barclay's Apolog y, page 46). We also contend that the Word of God is dynamic. The Spirit of God who inspired the words of Scripture also dwell within us. It is the word written upon our hearts, active in our conscience, and living through the one, Christ Jesus ("The Word made flesh") who speaks to our condition today. This is why we speak of "a listening spirituality" (Christian Faith of Friends, page 3).

We join Friends who hold the Scriptures in high regard, yet we are uncertain by what Friends mean by "Biblical authority." The Bible is subject to human translation, interpretation, and application. For centuries, "Biblical authority" has been used by political leaders to justify wars, slavery, genocide, colonization, and other ungodly enterprise. Most pertinent to our concern for North Carolina Yearly Meeting is the way people use the language of "Biblical authority" to pass judgment and condemnation on others, deny individuals of God-given dignity and grace, silence the voices of women, and implement a spiritual legalism of fear versus love. We also observe that some Christians who insist on "Biblical authority" practice it in selective ways. Many uphold parts of Scripture that support their positions, while ignoring other parts. What do Friends mean by "Biblical authority?" How will Friends determine what is authoritative? Who will make this determination?

Concerning Participation with Others – We are confused by strong objections Friends have about members of North Carolina Yearly Meeting participating with others. The "new committee" is asked to consider the general question, "Why do meetings feel compelled to participate with organizations outside of NCYM?" Quakers are not isolationists. Our ministries are enriched when we participate with other Quaker, ecumenical,service, and mission organizations for numerous reasons. It may be wise for our Yearly Meeting leadership to learn why our members are participating with the organizations that are now in question. It would be helpful to determine any threats these affiliations have upon the Yearly Meeting and discover if these affiliations prevent our members from fulfilling their responsibilities to our Yearly Meeting.

Concerning the Timeline – We are disturbed by the insistence that "unity" must be achieved now or by March 15, 2015. We remind Friends that the "unity" we seek is not agreement with each other, but it is "unity" with the Spirit of God. This is a prayerful process of discernment and reflection, which requires time and diligence. The "new committee" must have enough time to do this "worshipful work" well. We fear that the insistence and impatience of Friends may hinder us from bearing the fruits of the Holy Spirit as we work through the concerns. It seems to us that a Yearly Meeting which has just held its 317th annual session can grant the "new committee" and each other time to discern God's leadings in God's timing.

We remind Friends that North Carolina Yearly Meeting and its work belong to God; we are simply His stewards. God is the one who joined this body together, although imperfect and diverse, to reflect His glory and achieve His purposes. The opportunity is now before us to reflect God's power of love and spirit of reconciliation by how we tend to the differences and conflicts among us.

Therefore, we encourage Friends to: resist the spirit of aggression, ask forgiveness of those we may have verbally harmed or judged, and humbly yield ourselves to God and to one another. We ask meetings to stop making ultimatums of withholding support and threatening to leave our Yearly Meeting. We urge Friends to seek out opportunities to deeply listen and learn from one another, thus strengthening bonds of love and trust among us. We invite Friends to a season of prayer for our Yearly Meeting, each Meeting, our leaders, and those being called to serve on the "new committee." May we live in the virtue and power of Christ Jesus, who is our peace:

For he himself is our peace, who has made the two groups one and has destroyed the barrier, the dividing wall of hostility, by setting aside in his flesh the law with its commands and regulations. His purpose was to create in himself one new humanity out of the two, thus making peace, and in one body to reconcile both of them to God through the cross, bywhich he put to death their hostility. " Ephesians 2:14 -16

In the Peace of Jesus,

Greg Sheets, Presiding Clerk
Kelly R. Kellum, Pastoral Minister

Approved by High Point Monthly Meeting of Friends on
September 28, 2014

Letter from Spring Friends Meeting, Snow Camp NC, September 2014

We Friends of Spring Meeting, offer this statement in support of the solemn belief that actions do, of necessity, speak louder than any words, and illuminate the true character of ourselves and of others. Let thus our actions be that by which we are judged.

Unity within North Carolina Yearly Meeting of Friends United Meeting (NCYM-FUM): We believe that unity is best achieved by embracing of our diversity and, not through the cleavage of our association from others over doctrinal matters. We care not what an individual or congregation claims to profess, placing our highest regard on what they practice. For words, as we have witnessed, often mean little and are callously cast about by some. As George Fox stated, it is not what one professes that is of importance, but what one practices. We shall judge, and ask to be judged ourselves, by the actions of an individual or congregation. It is curious to hear others within our yearly meeting speak of unifying the meeting by use of exclusion and division, by attempting to cast out those with which they perceive do not agree with their absolutist interpretation of Scripture, their world view of social issues of the Day. Within the history of the Society of Friends, as with other faiths, this strategy has repeatedly been applied, only to lead to more division, more misunderstanding, and a distraction away from the true charge of our Faith. That true charge is to demonstrate by our ACTIONS, the love for our fellow persons after the example of Jesus Christ. As William Penn stated in 1693,

> The humble, meek, merciful, just, pious, and devout souls are everywhere of one religion; and when death has taken off the mask they will know one another, though the divers liveries they wear here makes them strangers.

We believe that each past schism has weakened our society and inhibited that cause of practicing the example of Jesus Christ. Each current branch of our Society has carried away some strength from the original Society, but has also abandoned some valuable attribute, to its detriment, to another branch. So it will be again if those professing unity through division carry the day. We embrace all branches of the Religious Society of Friends, that diversity begets strength and vitality as we strive to learn from and appreciate one another.

Askings by North Carolina Yearly Meeting of Friends United Meeting: What are "askings"? If the word is true to itself, it is something that is asked, not demanded. Our meeting strives to pay the amount of the "askings" requested by the Yearly Meeting which is consistent with our degree of use of the services derived from the Yearly Meeting. Over the past several years, approximately 30%-40% of the Yearly Meeting budget has been devoted to the funding of "Pastors' Benefits". Spring Meeting employs no pastor and has not done so for over a decade, choosing to adopt a tradition of Friends' worship that more closely resembles the historical manner of Friends. Our meeting has faithfully and consistently paid the 60%-70% portion of the Yearly Meeting "askings" that are not associated with the pastoral system, and apply the remaining balance to needs within the Yearly Meeting (such as Quaker Lake) and the greater Religious Society of Friends (such as the American Friends Service Committee, Quaker House, Friends Committee on National Legislation, etc.), and other needy causes. There have been expressions of concern by other individuals and congregations within our yearly meeting that funds are diverted to other organizations, such as

Spring Friends Meeting – Letter of Response, Page 2

Piedmont Friends Fellowship or Friends General Conference. These other organizations have no dues, no financial requirements for association, no "askings". Funds are not diverted from the yearly meeting "askings" to them.

Association with other Friends'organizations: Our meeting is a member of Piedmont Friends Fellowship (PFF) though we are not members of the Piedmont Friends Yearly Meeting that is being formed, choosing only to remain a member of the fellowship. As a grassroots, bottom-up organization, PFF does not have askings, dues or other financial requirements. It has no staff to support. There are no funds from our meeting being diverted from NCYM to PFF. Our meeting does not consider PFF to be a competitor or rival to NCYM. Our reason for having affiliations with both organizations is to bridge the chasm that unnecessarily exists between these two branches of the Society of Friends, each of which lacks a beneficial aspect of the other. While some members of each organization, particularly within NCYM, seek to widen this chasm and hold no association with the other, we seek a meaningful unity among Friends that such an affiliation can foster.

The "Founding Beliefs" of North Carolina Yearly Meeting: A common theme and quote in many of the recent letters from meetings has been their expectation of adherence to the "founding beliefs" of NCYM. This is a most interesting statement. For the record, North Carolina Yearly Meeting was first organized in the late 17th century, with the first formal gathering deemed a yearly meeting being held in 1697. The Religious Society of Friends and NCYM were founded during that century on the principles that each and every person could have a direct and personal relationship with God, that there was no need for what Fox and other early Friends termed hireling priests, our charge being to "walk cheerfully over the world, answering that of God in everyone". The increased emphasis on Biblical supremacy as compared to the leading of the Holy Spirit was not a founding principle. Robert Barclay, in his widely respected "Apology" (1676) on the foundations of the Society, went to great lengths to explain:

> From the revelations of the Spirit of God to the faithful have come the scriptures of Truth, which contain: (1) a faithful historical account of the behavior of people in various ages and of the many unusual and remarkable acts of God which they experienced, (2) a prophetic account of some things already past, and of others yet to come, (3) a full and adequate account of all of the chief principles of the doctrine of Christ which were spoken, or which were written, by the motions of God's Spirit at various times in treasured declarations, exhortations, and maxims which were given to certain churches and their pastors. Nevertheless, because the scriptures are only a declaration of the source, and not the source itself, they are not to be considered the principal foundation of all truth and knowledge. They are not even to be considered as the adequate primary rule of all faith and practice. Yet, because they give a true and faithful testimony of the source itself, they are and may be regarded as a secondary rule that is subordinate to the Spirit, from which they obtain all their excellence and certainty. We truly know them only by the inward testimony of the Spirit or, as the scriptures themselves say, the Spirit is the guide by which the faithful are led into all Truth (John 16:13). Therefore, according to the scriptures, the Spirit is the first and principal leader (Rom 8:14). Because we are receptive to the scriptures, as the product of the Spirit, it is for that very reason that the Spirit is the primary and principal rule of faith.

Spring Friends Meeting – Letter of Response, Page 3

It is our hope that NCYM-FUM does return to its "founding beliefs" and seeks a more comprehensive understanding and appreciation of the whole history of the Religious Society of Friends. Such an understanding might lead to the realization that the Richmond Declaration is a fairly recent document (1887) within that history which was produced by one faction within the Society with the intent to enforce conformity by that faction, with the result of creating more disunity within the Society that remains to this day.

Regardless of the efforts by some to enforce either strict conformity or separation– which only serves to divide, to ostracize, to cast our meeting chooses instead to continue to remain a member of this yearly meeting, to seek harmony, not division. We do not consider differences of beliefs among us as threats, but as opportunities for spiritual growth in a world full of God-created diversity. We shall remain. We seek to speak Truth to Power, and to act by the Golden Rule, after the example of Jesus Christ. We do not demand conformity of others, nor do we seek to be bound by expectations of conformity by others. We place little significance in professions of faith. We ask only to be judged by our actions. For as recorded in 2 Corinthians:

> Do we begin again to commend ourselves? or need we, as some others, epistles of commendation to you, or letters of commendation from you? Ye are our epistle written in our hearts, known and read of all men: Forasmuch as ye are manifestly declared to be the epistle of Christ ministered by us, written not with ink, but with the Spirit of the living God; not in tables of stone, but in fleshy tables of the heart.
> And such trust have we through Christ to God-ward: Not that we are sufficient of ourselves to think any thing as of ourselves; but our sufficiency is of God; Who also hath made us able ministers of the new testament; not of the letter, but of the spirit: for the letter killeth, but the spirit giveth life.

and reaffirmed by the Quaker elders at Balby in 1656:

> Dearly beloved Friends, these things we do not lay upon you as a rule or form to walk by; but that all, with a measure of the light, which is pure and holy, may be guided: and so in the light walking and abiding, these things may be fulfilled in the Spirit, not in the letter, for the letter killeth, but the Spirit giveth life.

Our statement should be disregarded if our practices fail to support it. The words herein contained are only as valid as the actions that consecrate or violate them. It is our endeavor to hold ourselves to such a standard.

Approved by Spring Friends Meeting 9/21/2014

Elizabeth Osborne, clerk of meeting

Spring Friends Meeting, Snow Camp NC - response to Questionnaire, November 2014

Spring Friends Meeting
Response to New Business Committee Questionnaire

1. In the last three years, has your monthly meeting ever failed to pay all of its "askings" to the yearly meeting? If yes, please explain why?

Yes. Our meeting strives to pay the amount of the askings requested by the Yearly Meeting, which is consistent with our degree of use of the services derived from the Yearly Meeting. Over the past several years, approximately 30%-40% of the Yearly Meeting budget has been devoted to the funding of "Pastors' Benefits". Spring Friends Meeting employs no pastor and has not done so for over a decade, choosing to adopt a tradition of Friends' worship that more closely resembles the historical manner of Friends. Our meeting has faithfully and consistently paid the 60%-70% portion of the Yearly Meeting "askings" that are not associated with the pastoral system, and applies the remaining balance to needs within the Yearly Meeting (such as Quaker Lake) and the greater Religious Society of Friends (such as the American Friends Service Committee, Quaker House, Friends Committee on National Legislation, etc.), and other needy causes. There have been expressions of concern by other individuals and congregations within our yearly meeting that funds are diverted to other organizations, such as Piedmont Friends Fellowship or Friends General Conference. These other organizations have no dues, no financial requirements for association, no "askings." Funds are not diverted from the Yearly Meeting to them.

2. Are the spiritual beliefs and operating practices of your monthly meeting in conformance with the NCYM Faith and Practice? If not, please explain why?

No. We believe this question may have been inadvertently worded incorrectly. Spiritual beliefs are individual beliefs. We as a meeting can't profess to know each member's and attender's spiritual beliefs, as we do not enforce a creed or have any "litmus test" that we impose for entering our meetinghouse door. However, it seems at least statistically unlikely, that every member's and regular attender's spiritual beliefs are in "conformance" with the NCYM-FUM Faith and Practice. Further, we believe very few meetings could truthfully say this. We do believe our operating practices as a meeting are in conformance with the NCYM-FUM Faith and Practice to the extent practical given our size.

3. If asked, would your meeting agree that the NCYM Faith and Practice, including the Richmond Declaration of Faith and the Essential Truths (   ), does an adequate job in defining the core spiritual beliefs of the meeting? If not, please explain why?

No. The Yearly Meeting was first organized in the late 17th century, with the first formal gathering deemed a yearly meeting being held in 1697. The Religious Society of Friends and NCYM were founded during that century on the principles that each and every person could have a direct and personal relationship with God, that there was no need for what Fox and other early Friends termed "hireling priests", our charge being to "walk cheerfully over the world, answering that of God in everyone". Emphasis on Biblical supremacy as compared to the leading of the Holy Spirit was not a founding principle of the Society of Friends or the Yearly Meeting. It is our hope that NCYM-FUM will return to its founding beliefs and seek a more comprehensive understanding and appreciation of the whole history of the Religious Society of Friends than can garnered from the Faith and Practice or the Richmond Declaration, which is a fairly recent document (1887), and was produced by one faction within the Society with the intent to enforce conformity by that faction, the result being the creation of more disunity within the Society that continues to this day.

4. Does your monthly meeting participate with any yearly meeting other than NCYM? If yes, please explain to what extent and why?

Yes. We follow the example of the Yearly Meeting itself and participate with other Yearly Meetings through many Quaker organizations such as FUM, FCNL, FWCC, AFSC, Quaker House, and the like. We are not members of any other yearly meeting, and believe that, to fully cooperate with FWCC procedures for Quaker census, a monthly meeting should only be a formal member of a single yearly meeting. We are members of Piedmont Friends Fellowship, which includes Monthly Meetings from multiple yearly meetings (as do many of the organizations listed above). And we have chosen to remain a member of the fellowship, and not to join the yearly meeting that is being formed. Our meeting does not consider PFF to be a competitor or rival to NCYM-FUM. We seek to bridge the chasm that unnecessarily exists between the two branches of the Society of Friends, each of which lacks a beneficial aspect of the other. While some members of each organization, particularly within NCYM-FUM, seek to widen this chasm and hold no association with the other, we seek a meaningful unity among all Friends.

5. For what purpose(s) should a monthly meeting contribute money to NCYM?

Money should be donated to the Yearly Meeting for maintenance of shared facilities, to offset the costs of gatherings for fellowship, and to support causes consistent with the testimonies of the Society of Friends. We believe the NCYM-FUM should return to its fundamental roots, follow the simplicity testimony, and minimize its use bureaucracy and paid staff.

Links:

Protesting Letters

Poplar Ridge Letter:
www.afriendlyletter.com/files/Poplar-Ridge-Friends-NCYM-FUM.pdf

Pine Hill:
www.afriendlyletter.com/files/Pine-Hill-Friends-NCYM-08-3024.pdf

Deep Creek:
www.afriendlyletter.com/files/Deep-Creek-Friends.pdf

Hopewell:
www.afriendlyletter.com/files/Hopewell-Friends-NCYM-08-2014.pdf

Forbush:
www.afriendlyletter.com/files/Forbush-Friends-08-2014.pdf

Plainfield:
www.afriendlyletter.com/files/Plainfield-Letter-ALL.pdf

Bethesda:
www.afriendlyletter.com/files/Bethesda-Letter.pdf

Responses:

Fancy Gap Withdrawal Letter:
www.afriendlyletter.com/files/Fancy-Gap-Quit-Letter.pdf

Spring Meeting "We shall remain" Letter:

www.afriendlyletter.com/files/Spring-Letter-Stay.pdf

Quaker theology is not explained by apocalyptic expectation and delay

By Hugh Rock

Introduction

Douglas Gwyn's thesis (Gwyn, 1986) that Quaker theology originates in imminent apocalyptic expectation has achieved a degree of influence. In its own right Gwyn's work stands as an expression of passionate personal conviction. Gwyn makes an empathetic bridge across the generations to relate his own sense of portentous times in the twentieth century to the circumstances of early Friends amidst the portentous events of the English Civil War. Through adoption by Pink Dandelion Gwyn's apocalyptic thesis has been incorporated into the framework of what I call the Woodbrooke interpretation of Quakerism that has been under construction for the past twenty years. It is this quasi-official account of Quakerism that is currently being presented to the public in the Oxford and Cambridge introductions to the religion (Dandelion, 2007, 2008).

This essay is written in the belief that the apocalyptic thesis is a diversion. To the extent that it is taken to offer closure on Quaker theology it stands in the way of continuing the search for a satisfactory understanding of Quakerism. A striking difficulty stands out. Even if Quaker origins were to be successfully explained as apocalyptic we would still lack an understanding of the theology. We would stand in need of an additional explanation to account for the fact that out of the "overwhelming number" (Baumgarter, preface 1999) of millenialist sects that have arisen within Christianity, Quakerism is one that survived. The placing of Quakerism as a commonplace occurrence in Christianity serves only to highlight the lack of identification of what is theologically unique about Quakerism.

Critical examination of the apocalyptic thesis is needed. To state my two objections at the outset: first, Gwyn takes the visitation of Christ as teacher to be the same as the second coming of Christ as judge. In essence Gwyn mixes up a Pentecostal experience of renewed spiritual strength with the apocalyptic Day of Judgement. The apocalypse in Gwyn's usage names something that is not the apocalypse at all.

My second objection relates to Dandelion's employment of an endtime/meantime dynamic to explain theological shifts throughout Quaker history. It seems obvious that there would have to be an adjustment from the excitement of immediate anticipation to the accommodation of delay and that this would show up as theological change. But this mistakes the distinctive psychology of the Christian apocalypse. In this psychology the *imminent* return of Christ, from its very inception, was mixed with the *certainty* of Christ's return. It is the certainty that provides the staying power in the Christian apocalypse and underwrites its special character that I name the "relaxed apocalypse." In this relaxed apocalypse the distinction between endtime and meantime does not drive any theological dynamic because the meantime, for Christians, already is the endtime.

The examination of the apocalyptic thesis is approached here first by looking at Gwyn's presentation. Dandelion's development of the thesis is taken up after this and more detailed consideration is given to what it is in the Christian apocalypse which renders it incapable of the explanatory dynamic presumed of it.

Gwyn's presentation of the apocalyptic thesis

Gwyn's attraction to apocalyptic was produced by a combination of four influences. These are: his sense of a present day approaching catastrophic culmination; his visionary inclination; the scholarly rediscovery of apocalyptic as the theological framework of the New Testament and the interaction of Christianity with Marxism.

In a retrospective Gwyn tells us of his own sense of apocalypse.

> I write [2004] as corporate and military interests have taken decisive control of the federal government of the United States. . .the Antichristian forces of finance-driven capitalism, multinational corporations and techno-militarism have reached a decisive stage of conflict with the needs of the world's majority of people. . .I was called to be a minister in September 1968. If ever there was an apocalyptic year in my lifetime, it was 1968. It was a crisis point of conflict and change in American society and around the world. That year included the Tet Offensive in

Vietnam, the Martin Luther King and Robert Kennedy assassinations, the May riots in Paris, the rampage of the Cultural Revolution in China. . .and much more (Gwyn, 127, 1986).

Gwyn's degree studies coincided with a time of renewed academic interest in apocalyptic, which, after its initial discovery around the turn of the century, had been put into the shade by Rudolf Bultmann's existentialist interpretation of Christianity. As Gwyn reports, "the growing scholarly consensus on apocalyptic eschatology as the organising principle of Jesus' and Paul's preaching was compelling to me" (128, 1986).

This struck a chord both with Gwyn's character and with his feelings of doom at "the buyout of American politics. . .by transnational corporate interests" (129, 1986). "I began to experience a profound unease. I felt something stirring both in me and in the world. . .I saw apocalyptic as the basis for a biblically grounded environmental concern. It is probably also true that the apocalyptic seer's panoramic distance and hallucinogenic intensity of insight matched my personality traits" (128, 1986).

These influences all come together for Gwyn in a Marxist interpretation of Christianity. Gwyn reports that he was "strongly influenced by Christopher Hill's Marxist analysis and revolutionary interpretation of seventeenth century Puritans and more radical groups"(130, 1986). But he was disappointed by Hill's lack of theological discernment in Friends revolutionary vision (130, 1986).

> "Marxists, such as Hill. . .have not grasped the true political meaning of early Quaker witness. . .The Quaker phenomenon as a mass movement with a well-organized network and a sweeping culture critique supplied *the key mediating term* between local praxis and state politics. The Quaker confrontation with the false authority of the clerical establishment and its magisterial enforcers made the Lamb's War the most serious threat to the new capitalist class, as it sought to consolidate its gains from the Civil War" (135, 1986).

It was against this background that Gwyn first read the *Journal* of George Fox. He writes that he was "stunned by Fox's apocalyptic language. . .it was a remarkable, seventeenth century parallel to Jesus and Paul's preaching of the kingdom of heaven, divine judgement and a new creation in present unfolding terms" (129, 1986).

For another person it is possible to read Fox's *Journal* without being struck by the apocalyptic language. It is true that the *Journal* is sprinkled with vocabulary taken from the Revelation to Saint John, such as the Lamb's War and the people in white raiment, but Fox's usage is not necessarily as Gwyn takes it. For instance, Fox's preaching characteristically warned people to repent because the day of the Lord is coming. "As I was going along the town, preaching and speaking, I warned the priest that was in the street and people to repent and turn to the Lord. . .I declared God's everlasting Truth amongst them and warned them to repent, and that the day of the Lord was coming on all sin and wickedness" (Nickalls, 91, 1952). Fox's prophetic relative in this is John the Baptist with his call "Repent for the kingdom of God has come near," (Matthew 3.2) and as Luke tells us "proclaiming a baptism of repentance for the forgiveness of sins" (Luke, 3.3). Jesus comes to Fox in the guise of teacher for preparation against that day, but he has not yet come in his capacity as judge of the living and the dead.

Fox's experience can be satisfactorily interpreted as a new occasion of Pentecost. The spirit of Jesus, working through Fox, gave renewed strength to a whole movement. I agree with Geoffrey Nuttall that the messianic aspects of Quaker writing are part of the "widespread extravagance with which language was used at this period" (Nuttall, 182, 1992). The fact, for instance, that Margaret Fell addressed Fox as "O thou bread of life" [1] does not lead us to conclude that she thought he was Jesus.

Gwyn is able to name a Pentecostal experience as an apocalyptic experience by making use of the ambiguous meaning of the word apocalypse. The apocalypse proper is defined by the Day of Judgement. It is on this occasion that God will reveal his overall plan for the rectification of the moral deficit of human existence. This God will do retrospectively by judging the dead, and by using his power to break the forces of antichrist. Theologically speaking the apocalypse is *a logical imperative of monotheism.* It is the answer to the problem posed by the writer of Job. Humans see that evil is rewarded and goodness is punished but if God is both good and all powerful this cannot be the final outcome of human life. God's moral purpose in creating the world must one day be revealed to us. The apocalypse represents that occasion.

The word apocalypse however contains the ambiguity that the Greek means revelation. The great apocalypse of Saint John incorporates this ambiguity in its title, "The Revelation to Saint John." Other revelations however may not be apocalyptic. It is this ambiguity that makes it plausible for Gwyn to decouple the second coming from judgement but nevertheless keep the name apocalypse. Gwyn uses apocalypse in this sense of revelation. He states, "Apocalypse as revelation itself leads us to conclude that Christian apocalyptic is most basically a matter of present experience, rather than speculation upon the future" (xxii, 1986). In this definition Gwyn discarded what theologically is signified by the apocalypse and substituted a spiritual experience of "the Word" under the name apocalypse. The result is a hybrid which seems somehow to combine an inward spiritual experience with an objective political event. The title of Gwyn's book *Apocalypse of the Word*, names this uncertain hybrid.

Does it matter that Gwyn swapped Pentecost for the apocalypse? Both are occasions of energisation which may be taken to have the same result in motivating Christian lives. The significant point is that Gwyn makes use of the apocalypse to take the religious high ground from which to complain about today's Quakerism in a way that would not be possible with Pentecost. The presentation of early Friends implementing the Christian Marxist political utopia of the Kingdom of God is used to berate today's Liberal Friends for lack of such activity.

The apocalypse, for Gwyn, frames a corporate vision of early Friends that has now degenerated into "individualistic relativism" (214, 1986). The apocalypse frames a "world-transforming fervor of early Quakerism" (216, 1986) that has now sold out in a plastic response to cultural religious norms. The apocalypse frames "the lack of prophetic power [which] is seen so acutely in the modern Society of Friends" (214, 1986). "Liberal Quakerism, that has proven ultimately unfruitful, partakes of an early twentieth century optimistic humanism that seems woefully inadequate to the problems of this nuclear age" (215, 1986). Gwyn is an ideological relative of Terry Eagleton for whom Christianity is a cosh to beat the self-satisfied new atheists with their "rationalist utopia" (Eagleton, 8, 2013).

A useful perspective on Gwyn's Marxist theology is provided by its relation to the mainstream of twentieth century liberation theology. Gwyn is part of the movement in theology which, ever since the Marxist attack on capitalism was first formulated, has wished to frame Christianity as the original Marxism. This was decisively stated early in the century by Karl Kautsky's interpretation of Jesus (Kautsky 1972 [1908]). Gwyn's immediate context of inspiration, as he tells us, is the liberation theology of the seventies (Gwyn, 134, 2004).

The Marxist Christian takeover of the Kingdom of God in liberation theology requires a particular theological manoeuvre regarding the apocalypse. To place that manoeuvre in context it is necessary first to record twentieth century theology's distaste for the apocalypse. Gwyn cites Ernst Käsemann as the scholar "who has done more than any other modern New Testament interpreter to further our understanding of early Christian apocalyptic" (Gwyn, xxi, 1986). What Gwyn did not mention is that Käsemann was dismayed that Christianity was born out of apocalyptic. Käsemann saw apocalyptic as a later imposition, alien to the thought of Jesus, which could not be made relevant for today (Käsemann, 1969). In this Käsemann obeyed the trend of twentieth century rejection of apocalyptic which began simultaneously with its discovery.

Albert Schweitzer felt apocalyptic made Jesus "a stranger to our time" (Schweitzer, 401, 1960). As a rational humanist himself Schweitzer welcomed the end of supernaturalism in a Christianity understood as a purely ethical religion of "Reverence for Life" (Schweitzer, epilogue, 1955). Klaus Koch surveyed the revival that Gwyn refers to in his book *The Rediscovery of Apocalyptic* (Koch, 1972). The English title misrepresents the impetus of Koch's survey which was to show the comprehensive theological embarrassment at the subject. The original German title *Ratlos* would have been better translated *Not a Clue What to Do with Apocalyptic*.

But supernaturalism aside, what made apocalyptic abhorrent to twentieth century theological ambition, under pressure from invidious comparison with Marxist social optimism, was the suggestion that the ultimate defeat of the forces of antichrist was God's prerogative and not within the capacity of humans. This seemed to concede all to Marx's complaint that religion is the opium of the people. A way out of this had to be discovered.

Faced with the insurmountable conclusion that apocalyptic did originate Christianity, what I call twentieth century 'apocalyptic resistance theology' took over the meaning of the apocalypse by re-interpreting it. 3 The crucial twist was made by Jürgen Moltmann in his seminal *Theology of Hope* (Moltmann, 1972). Moltmann pirouetted on the word hope and turned hope for God's initiation of his kingdom to mean hope for human initiation of the kingdom. Moltmann provided the answer to Christian Marxist dreams. He had formulated humanist theology's Socialist Kingdom of God.

Gwyn is part of this resistance theology. This rejection of the apocalypse and the conversion from God's action to human action is what Gwyn is doing where he claims Fox's declaration of the fulfillment of apocalyptic expectations. According to Gwyn "*Christ had come* to lead his faithful in new paths, thus setting up a new order and government. This announcement of a present spiritual return of Christ placed emphasis upon *apokalypsis* in its basic sense of *revelation*, transcending the Puritan inclination toward speculation on dates. . .etc." (Gwyn, 30, 1986).

To conclude the discussion of Gwyn, he takes the religious high ground of the apocalypse to make his complaint against liberal optimistic humanism. Ironically his theology turns out to be built upon that same twentieth century humanism in its appropriation of the apocalypse. 3.

Pink Dandelion's endtime meantime theological dynamic

Dandelion has identified four main theories of Quakerism in the intellectual record: the mystical experience theory, associated with Rufus Jones, and more recently Carole Spencer; the fulfilled realisation of the Puritan hope to be guided by the Holy Spirit, promoted by Geoffrey Nuttall and Hugh Barbour; the truly prophetic proclamation of the Christian message, promoted by Lewis Benson; and the theory of apocalyptic expectation, promoted by Douglas Gwyn.

Dandelion finds that "Gwyn's framework is compelling" (Dandelion, 5, 2007). Dandelion builds upon Gwyn's work by adding the factor of delay in the second coming. This proposes a dynamic of expectation turning into disappointment, a dynamic of original enthusiasm turning into quietism. As Dandelion reads Robert Barclay's *Apology*, it is a change from "the fearless sense of being a vanguard people" to emphasis on "fear and sobriety" (57, 2007).

Dandelion frames this dynamic using the shorthand of transition from endtime to meantime. It is this dynamic that Dandelion applies to explain theological shifts in the history of Quakerism. As he announces, Gwyn's framework is compelling, "particularly when laid out across time to explain the current challenges facing Quakerism (4, 2007). . ." The history of Quakerism is best understood in terms of its changing relationship to this founding experience of endtime and the necessary internal shifts which take place as a sense of endtime is replaced by one of meantime"(30, 2007).

My aim in this second half of the essay is to show how the distinctive psychology of the Christian apocalypse does not support this proposed dynamic. Dandelion's application of the meantime/endtime dynamic ought to be presented first.

Three themes are taken to be set up by this dynamic. Christian diversity is charted as a story of different perspectives on timing. It is charted by different approaches to the best way to wait and it charts a change of relationship out of alienation from "the world" to accommodation within the world (5, 2007).

Various results are put forward. The Quaker rejection of externals such as churches, priests and sacraments is presented as a function of living in the endtimes. These externals are considered to be meantime devices. They are "outward means other Christian groups had traditionally used to help humanity remain faithful both remembering the first coming and anticipating the second coming, in between times, i.e. in the meantime" (34, 2007). "Quaker worship was a second coming, or endtime liturgical form"(36, 2007) in which these past devices are rendered redundant.

The Quietist third period of Quakerism is presented as another meantime adaptation. "The Quakers moved from a position of being co-agents with God released from the possibility of sin to a group of people, literally world – and God – fearing, potentially preoccupied with their propensity to sin" (60, 2007).

The peculiarities of dress and speech are also presented as "meantime practices [by which] Friends helped each other remain faithful by visibly and audibly separating themselves from the world" (64, 2007).

My reservation about these endtime/meantime propositions is that they all have good alternative explanations. This reservation is compounded by a notable weakness in the theory. The sense of endtime had, in Dandelion's estimation, "already waned in the mid 1650s" (42, 2007). That is, almost as soon as the movement got started. Yet the endtime meantime dynamic is proposed to sustain shifts in theology for the next three hundred and fifty years even to the extent of bearing on "current challenges."

Sociology possesses a surer explanation of the process of initial hyper-enthusiasm evolving into lower levels of enthusiasm. This is Max Weber's theory of routinisation. Weber identified that it is natural for the energy of charisma, which founds movements, to settle into more sustainable forms. The omission of so insightful a theory, relevant to the Quaker case under discussion, is cause for suspicion of a thesis which proclaims that it is "informed by a sociological approach to theology" (1, 2007).

To give examples of these alternative explanations, it is in the light of Weber, rather than the evaporation of apocalyptic immediacy, that we can see the purchase of land for burials and the building of meeting houses (47, 2007). The abandonment by Quakers of liturgical forms is well explained by the focus of Quakerism on the spirit of religion instead of its man made forms. As Fox reports he refused to touch or taste the doctrines and commandments of men which he knew "perished with the using" (Nickalls, 168, 1952). Plain dress is one statement among several Quaker practices that refuse culturally constructed social hierarchies which contradict the equal value of every person. Barclay's omission of the second coming from his *Apology*, taken as evidence of his adaptation to the meantime, (23, 2008,

57, 2007) is explained by its irrelevance to his treatise. *The Apology* is concerned to stake out Quaker theology in relation to Calvinism. My impression from this series of alternative explanations is that the meantime thesis is generating the evidence rather than vice versa.

My central complaint, however, about the endtime/meantime dynamic is that it discounts the obvious explanation of Quaker history. The history of Quakerism is accounted for by the permanently unresolved tension between whether the religion is defined by the spirit of peace and unity, or by doctrinal tests. For me the whole matter is symbolized by the case of Hannah and Joel Bean, longstanding Quakers deprived of their status as ministers through doctrinal tests (Fager, p 53 ff, 2005). This tension surfaces as early as the dispute with George Keith (1638-1716). It runs through the dispute between Elias Hicks (1748-1828) and the Orthodox party. It runs through the dispute over Isaac Crewdson's doctrinal ministry (Wilson, 1990). It runs through the Richmond Declaration of Faith and the failure of the Manchester conference to endorse the Declaration. It continued to run through the Jones/Braithwaite formulation of Quakerism as a mystical religion in opposition to doctrinal statements. The matter continues to run with undiminished vigor in what Chuck Fager identifies as the "Ex-Quaker evangelicals'" distancing from the Religious Society by abandoning the use of the name "Quaker" for "Friends Church" (Fager, 138, 2005).

I call this tension between possession and profession the permanent schizophrenia of Quakerism. In this perspective the religion displays only one long droning theological period, not the "three distinct theological phases" (Dandelion, 3, 2007) engendered by the endtime/meantime scenario.

These anomalies thrown up by the endtime/meantime thesis are symptoms of a fundamental problem. The historical fact of the delay in the second coming of Christ does not have the explanatory power expected of it. This is because of its relative unimportance in the context of the overall apocalyptic scheme of which it forms part. It is this minor role that needs to be explained.

Dandelion cites Albert Schweitzer as his authority that Christianity was created as a religion of waiting. His perception is that "founded on the promise of the second coming of Christ and the end of the world. . .the history of Christianity has been about delay" (Dandelion, 5, 2007). Unfortunately Schweitzer, for all his genius, is not a good authority on this because of his blind spot. Although he discovered the apocalyptic origins of Christianity he dismissed rather than investigated the apocalypse. Schweitzer had no analysis of the particular psychology of the Christian apocalypse as compared, say, to the Jewish apocalypse.

In order to consider that psychology it is necessary first to dismiss the idea that the apocalypse is the catastrophic end of the world. As already stated, the apocalypse is the eventual revelation of God's moral plan for the world. The cataclysm described in the Revelation to John is one culturally limited attempt to imagine how that event would come about. John tries to envision the two features of transition that would be necessary to implement the wonderful new state of affairs. He seeks to show how the change from one world order to another could happen and he also imagines how the powers of antichrist might be defeated, be they the Roman oppressors in the case of his own church, or the empire of technomilitary capitalism in the case of Gwyn.

Spectacular breakdown has proved a compelling way to imagine that defeat. But catastrophe is not the essence of the apocalypse. Jesus, in his declaration of the imminent arrival of the Kingdom of God, also declared the apocalypse: God was about to implement his plan.

Christianity was founded at the moment that, after his death, Jesus himself was declared to be the apocalypse. God showed that he had a plan of redemption for the world through Jesus. God declared his hand on the apocalypse and assured Christians that the matter was at last under way. The imminent second coming of Christ which completes the event sits within this apocalyptic framework.

Yet *imminent* second coming is from the very outset mixed with the *certainty* that Christ will come again. Certainty is a close relative and fair substitute for imminence. This easy substitution means that the loss of imminence has little influence on the psychology. The matter is exemplified in Paul. Paul has to explain disappointed expectation to the Thessalonians because some of the faithful have died while waiting (1 Thessalonians, 4.13). But Paul himself seems untroubled because of his sense of baptism in Christ (Romans, 6.3) and "peace with God through our Lord Jesus Christ" (Romans 5.1).

Here the second coming is itself only a minor element in the Christian apocalypse. The major element is that Christ *has redeemed the world*. Christians have therefore already received the greater part of their apocalyptic inheritance. Their focus is on their joy and redemption in Christ. Compared to this the second coming has no more significance than the decoration on the apocalyptic cake that Christians are in the process of enjoying.

The psychology of the Christian apocalypse is that believers live in the assurance that God is taking care of the overall plan. In the meantime, which for Christians is also the endtime of history, the role of believers is to contribute their talents to the working out of God's purpose. Christians are energised and motivated by their apocalypse. The buoyant motivation generated and permanently sustained by the Christian apocalypse is the religion's attractive feature. This buoyant motivation belies the assumption that, disappointed by delay in the second coming, special compensations are needed "to help humanity remain faithful. . .in the meantime" (Dandelion, 34, 2007).

To state my objection to Schweitzer, Christianity is only in a formal sense a religion in waiting. Christ is the apocalypse *now*. The second coming is a coda. In practice Christianity is a religion of busy activity in the service of the apocalypse. To say of Barclay and his friends that they "were firmly pressing the snooze button of the alarm clock of the second coming" (Dandelion, 58, 2007) is to misinterpret the energising forces of the Christian apocalypse. Christianity has never been a religion of waiting or snoozing.

It is the context of the second coming that prevents that event having the explanatory power that might appear at face value. The scholarly attempts to extract explanatory power from the delay in the Second coming have yielded little result. Martin Werner's de-eschatologising thesis was discreditable because he sought to prove a superior ethical Protestantism over a superstitious Catholicism (Werner, 1957). Hans Conzelmann showed in exact detail how Luke displaced the imminent expectation in Mark in order to establish the mission of the church, but, for the reasons stated above, no deeper theological insight can be made of this (Conzelmann, 1969).

Conclusion

Where is the value of the apocalyptic thesis? It has appeal to a certain nostalgic spirit in today's Quakerism which seeks to recreate what it sees as the good old days of vanguardism. As Dandelion explains "Quakers ceased to operate as a 'second coming church' and joined the rest of Christianity in the 'meantime'" (62, 2007). "In the nineteenth century. . .Quakers took their place amidst Christianity rather than as its vanguard" (4, 2007)

There is a further dimension to the value of the thesis. It is put to use against today's liberal Quakerism. As Dandelion points out 'the meantime may be the *only* time for these kinds of [Liberal Christian] groups" (5, 2007). That is to say that Liberal Friends never will enjoy the full measure of spiritual uplift experienced by the first Quakers. More than that however "for those without a first coming a second coming makes no sense" (135, 2007). In terms of the endtime/meantime scheme Liberal Friends have "fallen off the chart" (135 and pictogram fig 3.1,

2007). The apocalyptic thesis is a device which portrays Liberal Friends in stark disconnection from early Friends.

To gain an overview of the apocalyptic thesis, it is best appreciated in its home environment of the Woodbrooke interpretation of Quakerism. The founding assumption of that interpretation is that Liberal Quakerism is an alien species with no relation to the origins of Quakerism. Liberal Quakerism is "the most radically deviant form of Quakerism to date. . .reaching out into new. . .interpretative identities that fly in the face of Quaker tradition" (Dandelion and Collins, 37, 2009). The apocalyptic thesis is a set piece in the Woodbrooke repertoire that proves that assumption.

Notes

1 Margaret Fox quoted by Nuttall from the Spence Manuscript.

2 A more detailed account of this can be found in (Rock 2014) chapter 1.5 *The Apocalyptic Resistance Theology of the Twentieth Century.*
3 In order to avoid possible misunderstanding I should make clear that I consider it natural that Friends may be inspired to political action by their religious convictions. My position is that there are many ways to support this theologically but we should not attempt this by rupturing the meaning of the apocalypse.

Works Cited

Baumgartner, Frederic *Longing for the End: A History of Millenialism in Western Civilization*, new York, St Martin's Press, (1999)

Conzelmann, Hans, *The Theology of Luke*, London: Faber and Faber (1969)

Dandelion, Pink, *An Introduction to Quakerism*, Cambridge University Press, (2007)

Dandelion, Pink, *The Quakers: A Very Short Introduction*, Oxford University Press, (2008)

Dandelion, Pink, and Collins, Peter, Eds., *The Quaker Condition: The Sociology of a Liberal Religion*, Cambridge: Scholars Publishing (2009)

Eagleton, Terry, *Faith, Knowledge and Terror*, in Hughes, John, Ed., *The Unknown God: Responses to the New Atheists*, London: SCM Press (2013)

Fager, Chuck, *Without Apology*, Fayetteville: Kimo Press (2005)

Gwyn, Douglas, *Apocalypse of the Word*, Richmond: Friends United Press (1986)

Gwyn, Douglas, *Apocalypse Now and Then: Reading Early Friends in the Belly of the Beast*, in Dandelion, Pink, Ed., *The Creation of Quaker Theory*, Ashgate (2004)

Käsemann, Ernst, *On the Subject of Primitive Christian Apocalyptic*, in Käsemann, *New Testament Questions of Today*, London: SCM Press (1969)

Kautsky, Karl, *The Foundations of Christianity*, New York: Monthly Review Press, (1972) [1908]

Nickalls, John, Ed., *The Journal of George Fox*, Cambridge University Press (1952)

Nuttall, Geoffrey, *The Holy Spirit in Puritan Faith and Experience*, University of Chicago Press (1992)

Schweitzer, Albert, *The Quest of the Historical Jesus*, New York: Macmillan (1960)

Schweitzer, Albert, *My Life and Thought*, London: George Allen & Unwin (1955)

Koch, Klaus, *The Rediscovery of Apocalyptic*, London: SCM Press (1972)

Rock, Hugh, *God Needs Salvation*, John Hunt Publishing (2014 forthcoming)

Moltmann, Jürgen, *The Theology of Hope*, London SCM Press (1967)

Wilson, Roger, *Manchester, Manchester and Manchester Again: from Sound Doctrine to a Free Ministry*, Friends Historical Society (1990)

Werner, Martin, *The Formation of Christian Dogma*, London: Adam and Charles Black (1957)

Book Review

Personality and Place, the Life & Times of Pendle Hill. Douglas Gwyn., Plain Press, 500 pages, Paperback. $20.00.

Reviewed by Chuck Fager

"Sometimes I look around and think, Pendle Hill is God's little joke on the Society of Friends."
– Janet Shepherd, former Dean

NOTE: From one perspective, it's a conflict of interest for me to review this book. After all, I'm described in it, because I was on staff at Pendle Hill for three years (1994-1997); more recently I spent nine months in residence there as a research scholar. Furthermore, the author is a friend of mine.

But having disclosed these items, there's a problem with this otherwise quite proper standard. In point of fact, legions of thoughtful Friends would be similarly compromised. Pendle Hill is, after all, a principal Quaker crossroads: hundreds, or more like thousands of Friends, from many countries and just about all the Society's branches, have spent meaningful amounts of time there, if not on staff, then at conferences, retreats, or as students, artists, authors, or other kinds of contributors. Surely there must be some perspicacious Quakers somewhere with no such connections; but life is short and deadlines are near; so Friends are advised.

Besides, the book soon became an absorbing read – and how often can one honestly say that about an "institutional history"?

Except Gwyn has not set out to write an institutional history. "My training," he says (vii) "is in biblical theology." Hence, his slant is both different and more ambitious: the book is "probably best described as *historical theology* [his italics]. It examines how religious ideas, ideals, and practices have evolved over time through a particular institution, interacting with changes in the wider culture."

Hence the subtitle, the "Life & Times" of Pendle Hill. Beyond the comings and goings, the highs and the lows, the book "ventures a *theology of history.*" [His italics again.] And in its eighty-plus years, Pendle Hill has been favored (and cursed) to have been through very interesting times, historically and theologically: not only wars and rumors of war, boom and bust, but also vast cultural changes in its Quaker constituency, with a theological evolution hardly less sweeping.

And yes, Doug Gwyn sets out to comprehend and grapple with it all.

Does he bring it off? Not entirely. But close enough to make this one of the most revealing and thought-provoking Quaker titles I've seen in a long time. And to repeat, I like projects with ambition.

❖

I can still remember when, as a new attender in the late 1960s, the appearance of each new Pendle Hill Pamphlet was a Quaker news event. Friends rushed (sedately) to get a copy, and passed it rapidly hand to hand. "Have you read it?" was the buzz query, followed by "Well, it . . ." Often discussion groups were organized to dig into the concise, but packed booklets. Many meetinghouses had special pamphlet racks for the series, which then numbered 150 titles.

In 1950, Gwyn records, the pamphlet series had more than 3000 subscribers, and thousands of individual copies were sold each month. That's a lot for Quakers, and the impact of the series was huge: it made Pendle Hill, even for many who never set foot on its campus in Wallingford PA, the conversational center of unprogrammed Quakerism, with ripples traveling outward far and wide.

Those were the days.

Gwyn notes sadly that by the middle of this past decade, the series' subscription list had dwindled to several hundred, even as the number of titles has passed 400, and new ones still appear several times a year. He insists the quality remains high; there I can't agree. Most seem to me eminently forgettable, as now, it appears, is the series.

The fate of the pamphlets is a capsule of the trajectory of the "life and times" of Pendle Hill Doug Gwyn charts in his pages. Opened in 1930 near Philadelphia, its founders included Friends from both sides of what was then a still-deep divide between Orthodox and Hicksite Friends, who saw the new center as a way of promoting healing of the century old split.

For nearly a generation, it thrived, and its influence steadily explanded. Besides the far-reaching pamphlets, Friends and others crowded in to take part in its programs. Gwyn quotes Dan Wilson, Director from 1952 to 1970, recalling to the board that Pendle hill was "packed, at times literally from cellar to rafters" much of the time during World War Two: "In all, over 80 individuals were bedded down on the same night . . .up to 90 in the summertime when army cots were set up in the screened-in breezeway . . . .Still others were farmed out for sleeping as guests of Friends in the neighborhood." (188)

Then again, in the 1960s, with better dorm facilities, students still came in large numbers: "the 1967-68 year saw 43 students in the resident program for one term or more." (241) And "Pendle Hill hosted 58 resident students the 1968-69 year, the largest group in Pendle Hill's history to date." (243)

But resident student class size diminished slowly but surely in the following decades: it was down to the teens per term when I was on staff in the mid-1990s. Last year (2013-2014) it was about half that; and for the current year, the program has been put on hiatus, its future uncertain.

Less material, but similarly striking, changes occurred in Pendle Hill's sense of mission and program. The founders envisioned it as, among other things, a "Laboratory of Ideas," a "School of the Prophets," and a "Haven of Rest." An initial brochure promised it would maintain a "rigorous 'graduate standard' of educational search," because

> "The path of religious and social renewal, it claims, is not 'through ancient authority or sacred tradition but rather through study, fearless experiment, and the sincere and teachable spirit on the part of each for himself.' The new center hopes to "make some contribution to the discovery and verification of truth in this realm of supreme value to mankind."

Today, in an alcove off the main room of its library, one can still find several shelves of venerable notebooks, filled with papers written by students based on their studies there.

But Pendle Hill gave no credits and awarded no degrees; the goal was righteousness flowing like a mighty stream, not a trickle of academic credentials. And by the 1960s, this practice was set aside, sloughed off by an unmistakable shift in student demand from interest in studying and changing the world to studying and changing themselves, and particularly their inner conditions.

The shift was noticeable as early as 1950, when a conference on depth psychology brought in one of the largest crowds of participants ever. And once the turn was made, it became seemingly irresistible. Staff and board members repeatedly voiced concerns about this. Douglas Steere, a philosophy professor and pioneer in interreligious encounter, became Chair of the Board in 1954, and in that same year he wrote to the Dean, Gilbert Kilpack, to protest that

> [L]etting people drift in their own way is simply not enough. ... Of course much of this is actually effected unconsciously by the permissive and enriching corporate life of work and worship and loving fellowship. But there should, I am convinced, be more. ... [Otherwise] we shall always be a second-rate, relaxed educational center where we cultivate the same kind of relaxed, well-adjusted-to-this-world sort of life that marks contemporary Quakerism to its shame, and that others will look at us with mild approval but without passion. (178f)

But Steere, who was often far away traveling and studying, lost that round to Director Dan Wilson, who was on the ground in Wallingford day in and day out. The next year, Wilson wrote in the bulletin to supporters that:

> There are no standards set up in advance as to what the outcome of a year at Pendle Hill should be. The hope is to see things in a different way. We are not primarily occupied with the outer improvement of the conditions of life, important as this is for those who do not have enough to eat. No amount of outer improvement alone will ever satisfy man. We are looking to that which has the power of altering our standpoint about others and their needs . . . .Pendle Hill is not a movement with a program. It must be a place where movements may arise or be strengthened, where people are allowed to come and go without becoming dependent.

Gone was any notion of "rigorous, graduate standard study." By the 1980s, Gwyn notes, "Pendle Hill's rejection of academic standards had generalized among some to become a reflexive distrust of intellectual activity."(335) And in 1960, the motto on the sign by the entrance to Pendle Hill was changed from "A Center for Religious and Social Study" to "A Quaker Center for Study and Contemplation."(x)

By 1964, Howard Brinton, long retired but still living and teaching on campus, noted that "Due to the demands and subjective temper of the times, there have recently been more courses along the line of psychology and psychiatry" at Pendle Hill.

In 1977, the noted organizational consultant Robert Greenleaf, author of the influential book, *Servant Leadership,* spent five days at Pendle Hill, interviewing and observing. He later sent a five-page letter to the Board with detailed observations. One of them noted that increasing numbers of students were arriving "wounded," and required much tending and counseling. He wondered, "has this become too much of a preoccupation"? He urged the Board to refine Pendle Hill's stated mission, with an emphasis on "leadership training," both for Friends and in the outside world. As Gwyn notes sadly, the Board ignored Greenleaf's counsel.

Yet concern over the distressed mental state of many students, and a therapeutic cast to actual programs, began cropping up with some frequency. In the 1980s, Gwyn notes,

> Many conversations between the board and staff in this period posed the question: "Are we a hospital or a medical school?" That is, is our mission mainly to tend to those on retreat from a depersonalizing society, or to send out personalist agents as healers and reformers? . . . As the problem went unaddressed, it fostered not only exhaustion but a similar sense of "woundedness" among staff.

But despite these concerns, the personal and inward focus only deepened, and the horizons of many participants became steadily foreshortened. In a 1986 Board report, an unnamed member was recorded as lamenting that Pendle Hill had become a "navel observatory." An effort in the late 1960s to turn the campus into a self-sustaining radical activist commune was decisively turned aside; the inward turn continued, accelerated as the art program, which began in a basement in 1960, finally moved upstairs in 1993 and became in many ways the center of campus activity. It has only been rivaled by an absorption with PH's large garden that has increasingly become something of an obsession. With this has come a nutritional politics that has turned composting and locovore veganism into the closest thing to an ongoing, coherent social activist program to be found there.

Ecology has also in many ways eclipsed theology. Gwyn shows how Pendle Hill's emergence was shaped by personalism, a once-influential philosophical-theological movement in U.S. Protestantism. Among figures shaped by it were Rufus Jones and Martin Luther King, Jr. Its adherents believed that

> . . . the person is ultimate reality, the only thing that cannot be explained by something else. Consciousness, . . . cannot be accounted for on an impersonal basis, but everything else can be described from the reality of the person. One might easily assume personalism to be individualistic and subjective, but it is strongly communal and political. [In fact, as one major personalist thinker argued], "individualism is the very opposite of personalism and its dearest enemy." [Another personalist insisted that] "the person is understood to be "theomorphic," or "in God's image" (Genesis 1:26).

That is, human personality participates in divine traits of love/compassion, reason/intelligence, and intention/action. The person is also "cosmomorphic," a microcosm of the larger macrocosm. Historically, personalism has generally been a Christian religious philosophy, affirming both theomorphism and cosmomorphism, but it may also be nontheistic or atheistic, affirming only the latter. In either case, personalism strongly affirms the inviolable dignity of persons. (3f)

Personalism has long since been displaced by other movements, though it still has presence in groups like the Catholic Worker. Yet among the Quaker constituency of Pendle Hill, the current successor, while hard to classify with precision, resembles an evolution of personalism into a kind of expressive, privatized seekerism, seemingly highly individualistic.

When Gwyn finished his book a few months ago, he spoke of Pendle Hill as being in a "struggle for viability." (457). The struggle remains in doubt as this review is written, in early 2015. If it does survive, it is likely to emerge different from what it has recently been, and even further removed from what its founders envisioned.

⁂

Howard Brinton once remarked sardonically (or was it wearily?) that "the idea creates the organization, and then the organization kills the idea". (275) Yet Doug Gwyn has not penned a jeremaid, aimed at simply lamenting Pendle Hill's decline, or forecasting its doom lest it repent. As he said, in *Personality and Place* he is undertaking a theological history, through the lens of this one institution, of both the Quaker community from which it emerged, and the twentieth-century American society in which it has persisted. Both the Quaker and the American parts of this landscape have been decisively shaped by capitalism.

Gwyn is very mindful of this backdrop, and takes what is essentially a Marxist view of it: capitalism turns everything into commodities, including people and ideas; and it runs in cycles, in which one capitalist center (usually an empire) rises has its day (or decades) in the sun, then decays, to be succeeded by another. In Pendle Hill's span, he sees the British empire fade, followed by the rise of American hegemony, which is now waning before a tide of eastern rivals.

This view he borrows from various writers, and we need not dwell on its sources here. Its real interest comes from what light, if any, it can shed on Pendle Hill's trajectory. To approach this interpretive task, Gwyn in his concluding chapter posits no less than nine frames through which Pendle Hill's history can be interpreted, ranging from the biographical, how lives of eminent figures like Rufus Joes and Anna and Howard Brinton shaped it; to generational, how the concerns and outlooks of those born twenty, forty, and sixty years after its founding vary recognizeably, with disparate impact on the institution; to administrations, how succeeding Directors and their leading board members wrestled with the problems of their day, and the questions of its future; to the succession of impressive writers who have left a paper trail of their lives and thought as shaped there.

These frames present a valiant effort to capture some of the conundrums of the Pendle Hill experience, and there is much food for thought in them. Yet, for a Marxist, there was one crucial frame which was not on his list, and its absence jumped out at me. I speak, in Marxist idiom, of the material substrate: that is, how (and by whom) Pendle Hill was paid for, from its beginning to the present. The answer, as best I can descry it, is provocative, and shows several distinct phases:

First, as the book makes plain, Pendle Hill was initially an artifact of Philadelphia Quaker capitalist philanthropy. As he puts it, "the dream of Pendle Hill was . . . a conscious intention among a few wealthy and influential Philadelphia Quakers." They talked about it, thought it was a good idea, had the wherewithal to write checks that make it possible, and did so.

Of this group, Gwyn suggests that D. Robert Yarnall was pivotal. Yarnall, from the Orthodox branch, was also a successful industrialist. Perhaps more important for today's readers to note, Yarnall and his peers, while outwardly modest, in keeping with traditional Quaker plainness, were not ashamed to put their wealth to work for what they considered good causes. Their involvement might today be called paternalistic; Gwyn notes that "Pendle Hill lore has it that [Anna Brinton] turned to Robert Yarnall at the end of a board meeting and said, 'If thou wilt write a check, Robert, we can pay the staff this month.'" (103f).

As these founders loosened their grip (Yarnall retired from board in 1954), Pendle Hill began a long and, it appears, often difficult transition to being a typical non-profit organization, which did fundraising to stay afloat: seeking out and cultivating new donors, with increasing support of technical means like direct mail. The transition was fitful: Pendle Hill did not have a capital campaign until 1977, in preparation for its fiftieth anniversary.

Yet for many years, this patchwork fundraising succeeded, and the campus showed it: more land was purchased, buildings built and renovated, the number of staff grew.

But then, by the 1980s, with student numbers falling, something changed. Those responsible must have felt that the money flow was guaranteed in perpetuity, because it became almost standard practice to expend more funds on generous financial aid packages than student fees actually brought in. The resident student program had become a kind of sacred cow, seen as needing to be preserved and populated no matter what.

There were staff members keeping the books who pointed to trouble ahead, with increasing alarm. Business Manager Denny O'Brien produced an overview of this pattern in 2000, disclosing that for every dollar of student fee income, Pendle Hill was spending $4.15, and was drawing on designated funds to cover this huge shortfall. Such tapping of designated funds for operating expenses was, he said candidly, "dangerous" and "scary." (361) Yet the pattern continued, even as succeeding recessions cut into income and forced painful staff cuts.

This habit of profligacy was well-established when I was on staff in the mid-1990s. I never understood why it continued, given Friends' long reputation for thrift and economy. It reminded me of a group of heedless heirs to a family fortune, running through their inheritance willy-nilly. Nor were they the only ones: now we know that in the same years, similarly wasteful and irresponsible management was characteristic of those two other legacy institutions nearby, Philadelphia Yearly Meeting and the American Friends Service Committee.

And now we also know that, just as a few unheeded Cassandras had warned, the party could not go on forever. In the late 2000s, all three groups hit the wall, and for two of them, the yearly meeting and Pendle Hill, the debris is still falling and the outcome is uncertain.

It is tempting to point fingers and look for scapegoats; and while Gwyn's text does not shrink from describing the missteps of leading staffers and board members, his text also makes clear that this crash was a culturally-induced one, not the fault of some convenient, departed executive.

In any event, the financial crisis at Pendle Hill arrived in 2005, with budgets slashed, staff layoffs, and associated trauma. In the decade since, Gwyn says somberly, "Pendle Hill continues to struggle for viability at the time of this writing,"(15). Moreover, its struggle for survival is taking a course that is, in light of staff outlooks for many years, a drastic departure, namely that of capitalist enterprise. While non-profit status remains, and fundraising continues, Pendle Hill has set out to remake itself as a conference center, catering primarily to non-

Quaker groups, touting its lovely grounds, quietist atmosphere, and (to some) highly esteemed cuisine. Profits (or rather, revenue) from the conference enterprise will, it is hoped, pay the staff, maintain the physical plant – and, with donor help, support some Quaker-oriented programs on the side.

At least in theory, this strategy ought to be, as the MBAs say, doable. Philadelphia is a large market, and Pendle Hill has 80-plus years of "brand identity" to build on. Moreover, as Gwyn points out in a case-study appendix, the conference center reinvention is one their British counterpart, Woodbrooke, seems to have managed successfully, to cope with a similar crisis of their own in the late 1990s.

Nevertheless, as I finished my research residency at Pendle Hill in the spring of 2014, safe harbor was still far off: more staff layoffs were pending; the centerpiece resident student program was about to go into suspension; and the financial reports I heard indicated that deficits were well into six figures, and breakeven was still years away even in the optimistic scenarios.

Suppose the conference center plan falls short? What if Pendle Hill as many of us know it turns out to be no longer viable? This is not a prediction; but even if uncomfortable, thinking the unthinkable may now be a responsible exercise. I see three options for post-Armageddon:

One is the equivalent of Chapter seven bankruptcy. Pendle Hill as a project is laid down, the property sold (it should bring millions), and the proceeds distributed to some galaxy of Quaker and presumably good causes.

A second would be a takeover by some nearby larger institution (say, Swarthmore College), which would turn it into their own conference center or a scholarly institute.

The third is a back-to-the-future fantasy: the tycoon manager of some One Percenters' hedge fund (or a techie app billionaire) happens upon it, is smitten, whips out a checkbook, and buys it, for preservation as a Quaker center-theme park.

A fantasy? Perhaps. But this is, after all, what happened to the *Washington Post*: Amazon.com's CEO Jeff Bezos bought it with his own pocket money – $250 million. And, remember – it is how Pendle Hill got started, as an artifact of unashamed philanthropy by people of wealth.

But again, none of these is a prediction.

Besides, despite the importance of this overview of profit and loss both for Marxist analysis and capitalist success, Gwyn's bottom line here is "theological history," not merely of Pendle Hill itself but of the Society of Friends that has populated and preserved it to this point; so what of that?

Here it is important to note that the founders saw Pendle Hill not only as a place for research into topics of current and future concern to Friends and the world. They also wanted it to be, as Henry Hodgkin put it, "a school of the prophets."

In one sense it surely was that in the first few decades: many key figures in mid-20th century social movements associated with Friends concerns such as peace were in residence there for a term, or a year, or two: A.J. Muste and Richard Gregg, architects of active pacifism and nonviolent action, were among them; Dorothy Day came through there, as did lesser-known but commanding figures such as Wilmer and Mildred Young, and Teresina Rowell Havens. Several of the many more in this company get welcome sketches in the book, which could help rescue them from an undeserved obscurity of time.

Yet few of the most prophetic of this band, with one exception, stayed very long. Why not? For one thing, like most prophets, they were restless, wanting to be out delivering their messages and stirring things up. This feature also made them less interested in the steady, usually undramatic work of community-institution building and maintenance. So the relative transience of so many notable figures is not a sign of failure on Pendle Hill's part.

Moreover, what was soon evident in the early years, remained so in the latter decades: Pendle Hill's leaders throughout repeatedly recorded their desire to be actively involved in racial reconciliation work, both on the campus and in surrounding communities. Yet the record also shows that Pendle Hill has had only fitful and sparse success at getting outside its base in an overwhelmingly white constituency. Rarely have such consistently noble intentions had so little real success; and the issue remains before it, unresolved.

The great exception to the brief tenures of those in its "School of the Prophets," was Howard Brinton. He brought together a contemplative personality with a clearly prophetic vision. Many of his writings still yield startling insights, decades after their publication. Further, with his wife Anna, the Brintons formed a team that was able to hold the young institution together and maintain an atmosphere of intellectual credibility as well as welcoming hospitality. The Brinton years from 1934 to 1950, were probably the acme of Pendle Hill's coherence and influence among Friends (recall that it was 1950 when the pamphlets were selling 3500 copies per moth).

There have been notable figures there since, but the list gets sparse after the tenure of Parker Palmer into the mid-1980s, now thirty years past. What has happened?

That same year of 1950, the sunset of the Brinton era, was also when a conference on psychology packed the house and marked the turn toward psychology, a path which led soon enough to the individual psycho-spiritual seeking of late.

This turn was not a programmatic blip; it reflected a sea change in the Quaker constituency. What was that about? Gwyn's account of the evolution is the best I have yet seen, but it outlines the mystery rather than solves it. Yet whatever the reasons (which Gwyn takes a stab at but are worth further dispassionate exploration), fewer and fewer Friends (or others) were (and are) willing to come to Pendle Hill and pay good money for programs on social justice or serious thinking.

I don't fault Gwyn for not having figured out all the reasons for this shift. He has done yeoman service in making its rise and course so plain. But there is one part of the larger picture where his book falls seriously short.

He says, as noted earlier, that Pendle Hill was begun by Friends from both the separated branches of Philadelphia Friends, and was intended to serve as one vehicle for finding ways to heal the split.

That goal was ultimately achieved. But unfortunately, after mentioning this ecumenical aspiration. Gwyn tells us nothing more of whether, and how, Pendle Hill actually helped bring it about. Indeed, he does not even advise us that the Board Clerk for the first 25 years, Robert Yarnall, was from the Orthodox side. And who represented the Hicksites? On page 104 we are advised that Clement Biddle headed the finance committee into undertaking organized annual fund appeals beginning in 1948; but we are *not* told that Biddle was a prominent member of the other, Hicksite branch; I uncovered that from other archival sources. Nor is the reunification of the two yearly meetings, in 1955, ever mentioned in Gwyn's pages.

This lack of followup is a puzzle and a disappointment. Reunification was one of the landmarks of American Quakerism in the past century; Pendle Hill was supposed to, and was uniquely-positioned to aid in the work. But did it? Some other historian must provide this answer.

In the meantime, Doug Gwyn has given us a rich and rewarding study of how an unprogrammed American Quaker venture has evolved and struggled for over three generations. The book also provides many insights which deserve further discussion and exploration.

Book Excerpt:

From *Personality & Place, The Life & Times of Pendle Hill,* by Douglas Gwyn

In Pendle Hill's Upmeads library hangs a print of Edward Hicks' *The Peaceable Kingdom.* Hicks (1780–1849) was a noted Quaker minister who lived in Newtown, Pennsylvania (about 45 miles northeast of Pendle Hill). He was also a painter at a time when Friends still shunned the arts. His great theme was the prophet Isaiah's vision of the lamb and the wolf, the lion and the ox, the leopard and the goat living together in peace (Isaiah 11:6-9), an image of God's realm on earth. . . .

Almost all [of the many] versions portray William Penn's 1682 treaty and land purchase with the Lenni Lenape (Delaware) Indians in the background. Penn is seen standing between his fellow Quaker settlers and the Native American leaders beneath a large elm tree. With his right hand, he grasps the hand of the Indian chieftain over a sea chest full of goods in exchange for land. With his left, he points to the treaty of agreement. This scene is brought into relation to Isaiah's vision by a child in the foreground who leads the animals with his left hand while holding an olive branch and pointing to the treaty site with his right. Hicks clearly viewed Penn's treaty as a historic realization of Isaiah's eschatological vision. Indeed, the early development of colonial Pennsylvania offers an inspiring exception to the generally unjust and violent relations between European settlers and Native Americans.

Hicks' paintings are relevant to the story this book tells, a story of *personality* and *place*. From a sermon preached by Hicks in 1837, we know that he interpreted the different animals in Isaiah's vision as various human personality types as they are realized and reconciled by the power of the light within. Thus, the peaceable kingdom is built upon the foundations of personal transformation *in community*. In the chapters that follow, we shall find that Pendle Hill, a Quaker study center near Philadelphia, was founded and sustained by a *personalist* philosophy, featuring a strong communitarian ethic.

Ten miles west of central Philadelphia, Pendle Hill persists today as a tiny residual enclave of Penn's "Holy Experiment."

The venerable American beech behind Main House was a mere sapling when Penn received his colonial charter from Charles II in 1680, and in 1682 when the Quaker John Sharpless purchased the 1040-acre tract that includes the 23-acre Pendle Hill property. Today a scion of Penn's Treaty Elm grows near that beech. With or without these historical and geographical reference points in mind, Pendle Hill is redolent with a sense of *place*. Stepping onto the grounds can feel like entering a force field that derives from several levels of community. A meditative walk around the perimeter path wends through a community of more than 150 species of trees. A community of worship is centered in the Barn, where Quaker meeting has taken place nearly every day for 80 years. The same room has been the site of an array of community meetings, classes, dramas, dances, musical performances, and lectures by speakers ranging from Jean Paul Sartre to Rabindranath Tagore and Dorothy Day. The Main House dining room is the site of endless rounds of shared community work and conversation. Nevertheless, the impinging presence of Interstate 476 and the desperate poverty of nearby Chester remind one that the peaceful *place* of Pendle Hill subsists within a larger socio-economic *grid*. Hence, the relentless processes of capitalist organization and differentiation of space will form the wider coordinates of Pendle Hill's story.

Thus, Edward Hicks' *Peaceable Kingdom* intimates a number of motifs that will be interwoven in the history that follows: Quaker-Christian faith and practice; personality in community; utopian social vision; nature mysticism; affinities with Native American and other earth-centered religious practices; spirituality and the arts; the search for racial justice and harmony; and the struggle to subsist and maintain a prophetic witness within a violent and corrosive economic system. This Introduction will establish the key coordinates of our study: personality and place within the historic conditions of modern capitalist society. . . .

Personalism, an all but forgotten stream of religious and political philosophy, was a generative force in several twentieth-century American, British and French movements. It has interacted with a variety of other philosophical streams, German idealism and existentialism in particular. Perhaps it is poorly remembered because it remained diffuse, or because the powerful forces of consumerism, the media, and technology have weakened the category of personality in our thought.

The Quaker poet Walt Whitman was the first self-described "personalist," in 1868. But what is a person? A grotesque protuberance of nature (Rabelais)? A laboring appendage of capital (Marx)? A twitching node of the market? A cog in the bureaucratic apparatus (Weber)? An organic prosthesis of the machine? Against all such despairing estimations, personalists posit personhood as the starting point of all inquiry. The French personalist Emmanuel Mounier writes, "the person is not a cell, not even a social cell, but a summit from which all the highways of the world begin" (1962, p. 114). Gordon Parker Bowne, founder of American personalist philosophy, suggests that the person is ultimate reality, the only thing that cannot be explained by something else. Consciousness, he argues, cannot be accounted for on an impersonal basis, but everything else can be described from the reality of the person. One might easily assume personalism to be individualistic and subjective, but it is strongly communal and political. Mounier suggests, individualism is the very opposite of personalism and its dearest enemy."

New personalist politics blossomed in postwar America, energized by figures such as Martin Luther King, Dorothy Day, and A. J. Muste. It found powerful expression in organizations such as the Southern Christian Leadership Conference, Students for a Democratic Society, the Free Speech Movement, and the Catholic Worker Movement. The anti-war, feminist, gay rights, and environmental movements were further outworkings of personalist politics. But as personalism expanded to become a counterculture, it was neutralized by the consumerist impulses of a burgeoning American economy. It sometimes turned toward a faith in childhood (beginning with flower children in the latter 1960s) emphasizing original innocence over the hard-won dignity of personhood, sometimes reducing accountable persons to helpless victims.

This study will reveal personalism to be the guiding vision in Pendle Hill's founding and first 40 years. In particular, we will discover the personalist thought and intentions of key figures such as Rufus Jones, Henry Hodgkin, Howard Brinton, Dan Wilson and Maurice Friedman. We will chart the decline of personalist vision over the second 40 years, but we will also recognize its continuing, unconscious influence in Pendle Hill's institutional logic and community life.

Personalism and Quakerism appear to have peculiar affinity: the traditional Quaker emphasis upon "that of God in every one" impels Friends to search for and engage the divine presence in the uniqueness of each individual, and to seek the will of God through communal processes of discernment. Whitman's Quaker background may have inspired his impromptu use of the term "personalist."

As postmodernist theologian Mark C. Taylor (1982, p. 89) has observed, once modernism had proclaimed the death of God, the postmodernist death of the centered self soon followed. (The humorist Wally Shawn quipped, "You ask me if I believe in God? Well, that depends on what you mean by 'me.'") The story of Pendle Hill offers a narrative microcosm of the larger struggle to reclaim and sustain personhood.

PLACE

Marxist geographer David Harvey (1996) has given considerable attention to place and the growing literature on the subject in recent decades. Like space and time, we construe place socially. Social entities achieve relative stability through boundaries and internal ordering, for a time. Such relative stability defines a "place." Thus, "Pendle Hill" can be located on a spatial grid of latitude and longitude. It can be located in terms of state, county, and township. It can be temporally specified by more than 80 years of duration thus far. But it is a place because various stories can be told about it.

Places are constructed within the flux and flow of capital circulation and expansion. They arise within territorial networks and divisions of labor. Concentrations of labor and capital produce differentiation, otherness, segregation, social tensions, and class struggle across space. Financial speculation pits capital factions against each other and generates competition between places, producing winners and losers. Thus, affluent Wallingford, Pennsylvania (Pendle Hill's geographical location) is situated less than five miles from poverty-stricken Chester, with the de facto racial segregation that typically accompanies class division in the United States. So, while the sense of place is powerful in Pendle Hill's internal story, we must keep referencing it to this larger story on the larger grid.

Joseph Schumpeter characterized capitalism as "creative destruction." Old Places are devalued and destroyed, and new ones are created in the same space. Since 1970, the rates of creative destruction and of competition between places have intensified 1n response to highly mobile multinational capital. . . . We shall follow the fortunes of Chester as a loser in this competition among places, alongside Pendle Hill's efforts to maintain itself as a nonprofit place within a capitalist system–an increasingly acute struggle after 1970.

SHIFTS IN THE HISTORY OF CAPITALISM

Marx teaches that capitalism alienates human consciousness. The commodification of nature into marketable objects for consumption and the commodification of human activity into marketable labor distorts our awareness of ourselves, one another, and the natural world. Therefore, macroeconomic shifts in the structures of capitalist formation can be expected to exert tidal effects upon the consciousness of whole societies. They also dictate the changing strategies employed by communities of prophetic resistance and revolutionary transformation. This study contemplates how shifts in capitalist society have affected the founding and development of Pendle Hill.

The work of Giovanni Arrighi (1994) highlights a particular shift found in the various cycles of capitalist accumulation, ranging from the Italian city-states of the fifteenth century through the Dutch, British and American cycles down to the present. In each cycle, capital interests find partnership with a particular military-territorial entity (state) that protects and furthers those interests. Marx notes a pattern in which phases of capital accumulation, which stimulate production and trade, alternate with phases of financial expansion and speculation. The shift from commodity production and trade to financial speculation and expansion marks the signal crisis of a particular cycle of capital accumulation. A *belle epoque* of dramatic wealth generation (particularly at the territorial centers of that cycle) accompanies the intense financialization of capital, to the neglect of productive forces at the center. That leads to a terminal crisis in which the particular symbiosis of capital interests and military-territorial power breaks down. Capital formation shifts toward a new cycle with a new territorial center (Arrighi, p. 1-8).

At the "commanding heights" of economic life, capital has an important "power of breeding"(Marx). But particularly in its financializing phases, it adopts a parasitic relationship to the everyday workings of the market (i.e., the conflict between "Wall Street" and "Main Street" in today's parlance). Arrighi goes so far as to describe financial capitalist activity as an "anti-market." It is important to make this distinction. Certainly, the market itself has morally ambiguous and socially decadent effects. But the most violent and oppressive potentials of capitalism reside at these highest "anti-market" levels.

This study of Pendle Hill will find three crises to be of particular importance. First, the signal crisis of the British cycle in the latter nineteenth century led to enormous expansions of wealth and global reach in the late Victorian and Edwardian periods. An ideological concomitant of this period for Anglo-American Friends was the flowering of liberal Quakerism, which framed Quaker faith and practice in new ways and began resisting more actively the rapid expansion of military-industrial complexes in Europe and America. This first crisis was foundational to the spiritual, moral, and social vision of Pendle Hill. The terminal crisis of the British cycle took place in the aftermath of World War I and the Great Depression. The American cycle of capitalist accumulation, already far advanced, becomes dominant from that point.

A second crisis of note is the signal crisis of the American cycle, the chaotic period 1968-73. This shift has been most trenchantly analyzed by Fredric Jameson (1991) as the birth of postmodernity, triggered by decolonialization and the neocolonial power of multinational corporations (global capitalism). We will note profound shifts in American culture, radical politics, and liberal Quakerism at this juncture. For example, an earlier, Eurocentric contemplation of world religions and cultures matured but also inverted into a more truly multicultural perspective and interreligious dialogue. The civil rights, women's rights, and gay rights movements of this period added to a multi-perspectival rethinking of liberal Quakerism generally, and Pendle Hill's programs and literature in particular.

Third is the terminal crisis of the American cycle over the past decade, which Arrighi predicted in 1994. The events culminating in 2008 appear to confirm the pattern of uncontrolled financial speculation, neglect of production, collapse, and a shifting of center (towards East Asia in general and China in particular). Hardt and Negri (2009) suggest however that the dynamics of empire established by the United States in recent decades augur for a multi-centered constellation of capital and military-territorial power.

In terms of Pendle Hill's history, we shall find the terminal crisis of the American cycle anticipated in a nonprofit setting in 2003-05, when the institution's venture into a highly speculative phase was undone by bursting financial bubbles in the stock market. Pendle Hill continues to struggle for viability at the time of this writing, during its ninth decade of existence. In examining Pendle Hill's current situation, we will consider the example of Woodbrooke, the British Quaker study center that has survived a similar crisis.

In the history of Pendle Hill. . . (c)ertain individuals may be more articulate or organizationally adept than others. But more than that, the group recognizes the exemplary integrity of particular personalities and the contributions they make to the meeting or the wider social order. Such personalities attain a certain substance–or "weight" in traditional Quaker vocabulary–that the group depends upon in its worship and decision-making life. We turn now to a few of the personalities that shone with particular brilliance at Pendle Hill in the Brinton years.

TERESINA ROWELL

Born in 1909, Teresina Rowell grew up, like Richard Gregg, the child of a Congregationalist minister. She studied Buddhist scriptures at the College of International Studies in London, completed a doctorate in comparative religion at Yale in 1933, and became an outstanding scholar of eastern religions. After teaching at Carlton College for three years, Rowell spent several months with the Itto-en ("The Brotherhood of the Single Light") movement in Japan, 1936-37. There she worked with the movement's founder, Nishida Tenko, who blended Buddhist and Christian teachings with his own insights. His practices of voluntary poverty had inspired a network of several hundred men, women, and children living in communities around Japan and Manchuria. Members volunteered to clean houses, public toilets, and streets, singing ancient songs as they worked. Tenko advocated a life of absolute repentance as antidote to Japanese culture's codes of revenge and honor. Never judge others; just go on with your own work and prayer. Itto-en does not denounce wealth but sets a counterexample. Through renunciation of property and service to others, one dies to self. Life is no longer enclosed in the body or the duration of a lifetime but joins the absolute reality, which is eternal. One enters the "World of Light."

Rowell visited Pendle Hill for the first time late in 1937. She stayed in the Brinton home, Upmeads. When the Brintons came downstairs for breakfast the next morning, they found Teresina scrubbing the baseboards (she had risen at 4:00 am). On New Year's Eve she set out on the four-mile walk to Chester taking no money. She found a broken broom along the way and began sweeping the streets when she reached Chester. This was the Itto-en method to make contacts and explore avenues of service and community building. People who passed by assumed she was drunk and left her alone. Eventually a man kindly asked her to come in from the cold and "it soon became clear to him that she was not drunk but only religious. So was he. His name was Moody Maguire, and he took her into the house to meet his family. ... They talked into the late hours, and she spent the night."

Rowell left Pendle Hill for three years of teaching at Beloit and Smith Colleges. But her New Year's Eve adventure eventually led to the formation of Pendle Hill's "Chester Unit" in August 1942, in which Rowell was joined by three former

Pendle Hill students: John McCandless, Dorothy Mahle (later McCandless), and Kathleen Laubach. Haines Turner (see below) also helped. In the abandoned Friends meetinghouse on Market Street, in the poor and congested riverside area of Chester, they established a combination retreat center, playground, children's library, and settlement house offering nutrition classes and other services. The Chester Unit forged a link between the serene suburban setting of Pendle Hill and the tough urban conditions of Chester. Rowell also taught world religions at Pendle Hill, but kept that identity apart from her ministry of presence and participation in Chester:

> Once she was sitting with a group who were deploring the limitations of their education. The confessional moved about the circle, one complaining that she had only reached the tenth grade, another the ninth, and so forth. Poor Terry waited in anguish. Would she have to admit to a doctorate from Yale and a berth on the Smith College faculty? How strange, even treasonable it would seem to them! So keen was her distress that it showed in her face. Presently a kind hand touched her arm. "Never mind, dearie," whispered the woman next to her, "I couldn't get through high school either."

Mather tells how Rowell had learned to participate–not reform–in a rural mining community in the Midwest in the 1920s:

> The key to her participation lay in a blue silk dress. It was not her own, her wardrobe then consisting largely of seersucker-a sturdy, no-iron fabric which she wore on every occasion, including attendance at church. This was too much for the miners' wives who, no matter how poor, always wore silk on Sunday. When one woman offered her a blue silk dress, saying she "might feel more comfortable in it," Terry got the message. Seersucker did not show sufficient respect. Though a silk dress was not her own way of showing respect she saw that it was theirs. So she took the proffered garment and wore it. (Mather, p. 41)

Teresina Rowell described the Chester project in *Building Tomorrow: Some Quaker Explorations*, a booklet published in 1943 by the Social Order Committee and Committee on Economic Problems of Philadelphia Yearly Meeting (Orthodox). Chapters were written by various authors associated with Pendle Hill at that time, including William Simkin on industrial democracy, Bayard Rustin on racial reconciliation, Wilmer and

Mildred Young on participation in rural life, Bernard Walton on Quaker meeting life, Bernard Waring on private business, and Teresina Rowell on community with city workers.

Rowell begins with an epigraph from Nishida Tenko suggesting that all we can do to end the world's struggles for more is to repent from our own material possessions. After describing her life among shipbuilders and other working families in Chester, she offers a query: how do we overcome class barriers? We can begin now, she answers, by renouncing our own privilege and living more cooperatively in community. This "socializes" our property, time, and training. Rowell explains how the group living together in Chester pooled their small incomes, drawing out for modest personal expenses, but consulting with the group on larger ones. They considered neither money nor time as their own to spend. They all worked part-time, some in their old professions, others taking on manual labor, others using their earlier training to help working families. At the time of her writing, no group projects had developed so far, except to help an African-American Boy Scout troop clear a playground for use. Most of their time was spent in employment and housework. They began to understand why workers did not feel like coming to meetings in the evening!

They entertained drop-ins from the neighborhood, discussed local politics, and borrowed things from one another. Friends from Pendle Hill also visited and participated, seeing firsthand the harm that mechanized civilization inflicts upon working people in the form of low wages and dangerous working conditions. Their children grow up without religious or cultural influences, which creates further social problems. Our continued acquiescence to these inequities will frustrate all attempts to build a more brotherly society after the war. Religiously-concerned citizens are needed to tackle these problems first-hand. "Trying to bridge the gap between racial and economic groups, which now look at each other through prejudiced stereotypes, seems to us a much-needed function, particularly for Friends to perform."

Chester was growing rapidly in the war years. Shipbuilding and other defense-related industries in Chester drew large numbers of workers. The African-American population expanded to one-third of the city's total population by the late 1940s. Their community experienced especial tension with new Eastern European arrivals, who competed for the same jobs and absorbed the racial prejudices of the wider American culture. Despite their comprising a sizable portion of the local population, Chester's black citizens were hedged in by an oligarchic political machine. But starting on V-J Day, black parents launched an attack on Chester's segregated and unequal school system, and soon won a desegregation decision in court–ten years ahead of the national civil rights movement.

During the late 1940s the young Martin Luther King, Jr., a recent graduate from Atlanta's Morehouse College, was a student at Chester's Crozer Theological Seminary, where he began to study Gandhian nonviolence. That interest may have led him into connections with Pendle Hill or the Chester Unit, but there is no surviving evidence of contact. Besides Gandhian nonviolence, personalism was another interest King shared in common with Pendle Hill. His studies with African American personalist George Washington Davis at Crozer led him on to doctoral work at Boston University, the center for American personalist theology. King would later reflect that personalist idealism became

> my basic philosophical position. Personalism's insistence that only personality – finite and infinite – is ultimately real, strengthened me in two convictions: it gave me metaphysical and philosophical grounding for the idea of a personal God, and it gave me a metaphysical basis for [my belief] in the dignity and worth of all human personality.

Some biographers have suggested that his academic interest in personalism grew out of the generally personalist tone of African American culture (see Burrow, 1999, pp. 78, 266).

Rowell also wrote penetratingly on the challenges of community life. In "Unifying Disciplines for the Religious Community" (*The Journal of Religious Thought*, 1944) she distills her experiences with Itto-en, Pendle Hill, and the Chester Unit. She notes the currently "high mortality rate" among cooperative houses, and cautions that intentional community is primarily a state of mind, a shared sense of symbols, attitudes, and aims. When this inner unity is lost, communal sharing quickly degenerates. Communal movements of the past were not usually born of a desire to start a community, but through shared experiences of a new spirit and pattern of life, shown by the example of a saint or savior, such as the Buddha, St. Francis, or Nishida Tenko. The sense of identification is stronger than the fear of loss or failure. The usual human wants are transformed by the glimpse of a better life.

But that transcendent unity is easily lost. How can the original redirection of the will be kept alive? What specific disciplines keep human wills oriented together? First, Rowell answers, regular reminders of the community's purpose are needed, such as the Church's ritual celebration of the Lord's Supper, the Jewish liturgical calendar, and the use of music, art, or silence. She mentions in particular Pendle Hill's Summer

Session of 1943, when a group discipline of silence, shared work, devotional reading, and worship at regular intervals produced a strong sense of unity. Participants still felt bonded together well after they had scattered at the end of the session. (Rowell was a catalyst inestablishing silent retreat times at Pendle Hill in this period.)

Also crucial is the power of example, often set by a community director or leading teacher. Although CPS camps and pacifist cooperative farms are developing more broadly shared decision-making, this sometimes proves harder than simply submitting to the authority of a spiritual director. It may be harder to trust that the group's decisions are right. Meanwhile, ceremonies and recreation are important to building group cohesion. In the final analysis, however, group consciousness cannot be deliberately created by human effort. It is a byproduct of working together, not something sought as an end to itself. Ultimately, it is a matter of God's grace. It is God who calls and gathers us into community.

In 1945, Rowell wrote an article for The *Friends Intelligencer* on the Itto-en movement (cited at the beginning of this section), which appeared the week Hiroshima was bombed. Joseph Havens was moved by the article and wrote to her, asking if they could meet. She responded that she was too busy, but he eventually he came to see her anyway. They were married early in 1947. After another year at Pendle Hill and Chester they left with their baby daughter for California, where Joe studied with Fritz Kunkel and Teresina returned to brief periods of academic teaching. Upon the Havens' departure, the Brintons reflected that Terry's "vivid outlook on individuals and society, East and West, her unusual scholarly and deep dedication, have added breadth, zest, and devotion to our life at Pendle Hill. For many years hers was the ministry which kindled into living fire the gift of God" (annual report, *Bulletin* #85, October 1948).

MILDRED AND WILMER YOUNG

[A]mong those most affected by Richard Gregg's teaching [on nonviolent action] at Pendle Hill were Wilmer and Mildred Young. Wilmer had grown up among Conservative Friends in Iowa and had attended the Scattergood Boarding School. After graduating from Haverford College, he taught at the Friends Boarding School in Barnesville, Ohio, maintained by Ohio Yearly Meeting (Conservative). There he met Mildred Binns, who had also grown up a Conservative Friend. Mildred's early faith was informed mainly by tradition: Scripture was read aloud but never interpreted, following the Quaker belief that the Spirit in each person must do the interpretation. When she and Wilmer were married in 1922, they rebelled from their Quaker roots and traditional Christian faith. Mildred later reflected that her traditional upbringing gave her strength during this period to hold everything religious in abeyance until living experience could renew her faith on solid ground.

Wilmer strongly believed that service to God takes the form of service to humanity. Radical social engagement came less easily for Mildred, but she came to realize "it was the poor who were to be my teachers ... it was the knowledge of their need that was the lantern in my hand". They worked for the AFSC in Poland in 1924, where they saw desperate need for the first time. Returning to America, they taught the next 12 years at the Westtown Friends Boarding School, near Pendle Hill. Meanwhile they also worked with miners in Kentucky and led the first AFSC work camp in 1934. They were further radicalized by Richard Gregg's teaching and example at Pendle Hill. They adopted intentional poverty for the next 20 years, beginning with their move in 1936 to the Fellowship of Reconciliation's Delta Cooperative Farm in Mississippi.

Mildred and Wilmer had already learned at the work camps that true leadership comes not from above or from afar, but alongside, at close quarters. It must engage the whole person–joints and muscles, not just eyes and ears. Mildred also realized later that "the hand that gives must touch the hand that receives." In modern years, much service work and charity pass through large, less personal organizations, but without direct contact between giver and receiver, neither is fed spiritually. Mildred had to learn the importance of spending time with people, not just helping them. "It is easy to waste time but hard to be generous with it". During the autumn term of 1938 at Pendle Hill, Mildred gave three talks on her unfolding experience and learning. These were collected and edited to become her first Pendle Hill Pamphlet, *Functional Poverty* (#6, 1939).

The Youngs spent three years growing cotton at the Delta Cooperative Farm with evicted sharecroppers. They moved in 1939 to the AFSC's Little River Farm Community in western South Carolina to work with black and white tenant farmers. They stayed the next 15 years, farming with their three children and teaching soil conservation, care of woodlands, crop diversification, household management, and childcare. Twenty-two local families became owners of their own homes, farming cooperatively. Over time, however, the Youngs saw participants grow further apart as they became more prosperous. The Youngs chose to stay poor.

Mildred preferred the term "poverty" over "simplicity," which she found more ambiguous, prone to becoming more a matter of style than substance. Quoting the personalist Catholic Worker Peter Maurin, Young stressed the need to "create conditions in which it is easier for a man to do good." Voluntary poverty places men and women in a situation where they are compelled to be good to one another in community. It becomes easier to gain the purity of heart that wills one thing, to renounce the mental states of greed and resentment. In true poverty of spirit we come within sight of the cross, where Jesus took upon himself "the whole burden of hope, and laid on us, to bear in our degree, the burden of hope for humanity".

Mildred Young followed Richard Gregg in identifying war as integral to the unjust and exploitative societies that wage it. In 1942 she reflected mordantly that the war effort was like a game played with someone who is ill – who cares who wins or loses. You play to get your mind off the illness.

Nothing is proved or accomplished in war and there is no logical next step when it is over. By contrast, small-scale farming integrates the personality with other people, animals, and the land itself. Finding fulfillment in the life of poverty takes time: there are many unclean spirits of modern life to be cast out, through "prayer and fasting." Like the vocations in the Roman Catholic Church, this vocation requires a long novitiate.

Writing during a bad crop year on their farm, Young reflected, "the farmer is insured by hope against all failure," always focusing on the next growing season. "[W]e are all knit together in the unending chain of creation and growth and interaction . ... As long as these bonds remain and we know ourselves continuous with the whole of life, we cannot fail. The knowledge of this unity makes us whole. We are insured by life" (p. 3). Only by cutting ourselves off from community with the whole creation are we perishable. Mildred Young's personalism embraced all life and contemplated the interdependence of humans with animals and the entire created universe. "And underneath this stupendous symbiosis, the everlasting arms".

The Youngs left the South in 1955 to join the staff at Pendle Hill, where they taught nonviolent methods of responding to war, poverty, and racial injustice for the next five years. Mildred Young's seven Pendle Hill Pamphlets, from 1939 to 1971, are among the most outstanding of the series. In each she integrates hard-won practical experience with larger social insights, a deepening Christian witness, proto-ecological vision, and penetrating challenges to Friends in their comfortable lifestyles.

A Convergent Model of Renewal: Remixing the Quaker Tradition in a Participatory Culture. C. Wess Daniels. Pickwick/Wipf and Stock Publishers. 224 pages. Paper, $21.60.

Reviewed by Chuck Fager

There's more than little *déjà vu* about *A Convergent Model of Renewal*. Quakerism, Wess Daniels argues, will be renewed by the coming together of Friends from the fringes of the various branches, particularly younger members and seekers. Or as he puts it: "It could be said that convergent Friends signal the emergence of a new Quakerism that transgresses the boundaries of any one Quaker group." (D 16f)

Why *déjà vu?* Because such a sentence (minus perhaps the "transgresses") could have been written in the 1920s, either for young Friends in the Northeast, or the "All-Friends Conference" of 1928. Then again in the late 1940s through the 1950s for gatherings of Young Friends of North America (YFNA). Or in 1977 for the all-branch Friends Gathering in Wichita. Or in 1985 and 2005, for the two World Gatherings of Young Friends, in Greensboro, North Carolina and Lancaster, England. Nor let us forget the YouthQuakes of the '80s & '90s. (And there were more.)

So such "New" Quakerisms have been heralded many times in North America in the past century.

These events and groups faced various obstacles, but were by no means all failures. For instance, they helped bring together the fractured Hicksite and Orthodox branches in the East, which was no mean feat. Many collaborated (albeit under some compulsion) as conscientious objectors in World War Two. And without fanfare, some participants from various branches stayed in touch; a few even married; others worked together as way opened, in war and peace.

Still, in two major respects these twentieth century pioneers did fail – first, by failing to be remembered; and we find this book continuing their erasure by looking back to the 1660s and the 1670s, but skipping over this long chain of more recent efforts as if it had never been forged. Too bad.

Their second "failure" was even more egregious, and the more offensive because unavoidable: the "New" Quakers of the 1920s grew old, as, in turn, did all their successors. And as those readers who are now "old" will know, we become steadily more invisible as the decades pass.

Ah well, in our consumer culture, memory is one of the major consumables, and remembering much beyond last week's mass-produced version of "reality" an increasingly rare act of both resistance and dogged, unremitting effort. Also, the seeming fixation on youth, as most ex-youth have now learned, has more to do with making sure each new cohort is thoroughly conditioned and embedded in the market's matrix before they can make other arrangements.

And so we come to the newest "New Quakerism," that of "Convergent Friends," a trend that has been much talked about in recent years. There have been gatherings, blogs, enthusiastic articles, and not a little ageist snark at us Old Fart Friends and the screwed up Quaker mess we dumped in their laps. The innovation here, as Robin Mohr, who is credited with coining the term, describes it, is that they are bringing together "Friends from the politically liberal end of the evangelical branch, the Christian end of the unprogrammed branch, and the more outgoing end of the Conservative branch." (17)

Which is to say, they're doing pretty much what their predecessors did, with a few novel twists such as social media. Their openness to LGBT folk might seem utterly new; yet pushing the envelope is part of the pattern, and in the past century, restless young Friends have had plenty of envelope to push.

While it's too bad the convergents generally don't seem to know or care much about earlier efforts, this doesn't mean their impulses are unwarranted. After all, many of the jabs at us older Friends are on the mark: despite our labors and those of all the earlier bands of New Quakers, previous "renewals" have not stopped many yearly meetings from hemorrhaging members. And even though some Friends from the fringes of various branches have scaled the walls of division, most of the barricades outside the Hicksite-Orthodox orbit not only remain, but many even seem higher than ever, as numerous American Quaker bodies seem to be facing a new round of divisions.

This is the case in Daniels' own Northwest Yearly Meeting, where the current fault lines involve efforts to ward off any acceptance of LGBT persons, squelch any loosening of their evangelical doctrinal stance; and push out the voices of such reforms. The outcome of these struggles is by no means clear.

Daniels does not address the Northwest controversy specifically. But indirectly the agenda is clear: his convergents think it's time for these doctrines to be re-examined and "remixed" in a looser, more open, but still somewhat recognizable form by a new generation, and as part of that process, for programmed Friends to get past the insistence on traditional heterosexuality as the only permissible way of life and love.

While reading his book, I kept wondering if his arguments seemed likely to sway any of those now moving to expel heretics and sexual subversives from his and other groups. It's not his fault that I doubt it very much; but I do.

Then what about broader "renewal"? Can the Convergent Friends reverse the decline of numbers and perceived vitality in American Quakerism? Several of the more vocal convergents, whom Daniels lists, have occupied some key slots in the Quaker infrastructure: the editorship of Friends Journal, FWCC's Section of the Americas, a handful of yearly meeting staff jobs, and in the Quaker Volunteer Witness, a promising startup project. For all these, the jury is still out. With Daniels' book, they hoped to gain a theoretician and a theory.

The underlying schema for his program is largely drawn from the work of philosopher Alasdair Macintyre, who sees "authentic" renewal coming from re-examination of a tradition's history & key texts by insurgent "apprentices" who take it seriously but who are ready to revise and "remix" it to cope with new cultural and historical challenges. (Kudos and heartfelt thanks to Daniels for using "remix" instead of the thoroughly worn-out and utterly unconvincing "transformation.")

Daniels aims this counsel mainly at his evangelical establishmentarians whose grip on Quakerism's actual history and "distinctives" is often so loose as to slide seamlessly into the Baptist or generic Wesleyan camps. But it applies just as well to the many liberals whose Quaker holy trinity boils down to Penn, Prius & NPR.

Daniels situates his new New Quakerism in today's burgeoning "remix" and "participatory culture," replete with social media. His treatment of this new environment is illuminating (if too long and repetitious). For him, the more Quaker remix, the more slicing and dicing of traditions into new sacred salads, the better, it appears.

I wonder. After a lot of razzmatazz about new media and "contextual theology," the New Quakerism here looks mostly like a call for an evangelicalism with a looser grip on doctrine and an openness to LGBT persons; or a liberalism whose "spiritual journey" chugs into a ghost town populated by dust-and-cobweb covered artifacts of Christianity and the Bible, presided over by a sheriff with initials JC, who turns out to be not quite the zombie the pilgrims were expecting.

That would be fine with me. But can the convergents bring it off? Unfortunately, there is as yet no hard data about how widespread convergent sentiment is, or if it has had any actual impact. And to fill this yawning blank, Daniels stakes his case on a single "real-life" example, that of Freedom Friends Church (FFC) in Salem, Oregon. He examines it in detail, and to speak plainly, to me it came across as too weak a reed to bear the weight of his remixing ardor.

Freedom Friends is an independent, "semi-programmed, lightly pastored" church that was founded by two ex-members of Northwest Yearly Meeting who wanted a church that would be open to LGBT folks and other outsiders, but remain identifiably Christian. And to be sure, FFC has been an interesting experiment, and I wish them well.

But Daniels presents it as the new convergent epitome. He sets up the profile by citing the dilemma articulated by John Punshon in his 1987 book *Reasons for Hope* about the decline in many evangelical Friends groups. Punshon said they're failing because they don't fill a "distinct niche" in the American religious ecosystem. Yet, he insisted, there was indeed such a niche – a big one – just waiting to be filled, with Quaker "distinctives." Wess identifies FFC as this distinctive turnaround niche-filler.

Except it isn't: FFC started small, it has stayed small, and is declining, as indicated by its recent "State of the Church" reports. In the profile, Daniels featured a key member in a dramatic, several-page "convincement narrative." Unfortunately, as the latest FFC report notes, that member is now gone: she committed suicide. There's hardly anyone left.

Moreover, FFC's high social media profile (Facebook page, website, blog, fast-selling Faith & Practice) is, well, not exactly special in 2015 – Friends meetings and churches all across the spectrum have them, and some (mainly among the trendier evangelicals) have plenty more gadgetry besides.

Indeed, while his treatment of today's burgeoning "remix" and "participatory culture" is in many ways admirable, I wish Daniels had pushed it further, into some critical reflection on this frenetic, totalizing environment: is it really the church's role to jump right in and get "contextualized" (i.e., swallowed up) in it? Or is this galloping techno-tsunami due for a word of judgment and challenge, along with the rest of a fallen creation? I hear occasional ambivalence and hesitation from other "Convergent" voices about all this; but not in these pages. Yet I still wonder.

Of course, experiments don't need to "succeed" to be useful. And FFC's salient features have been these: its independence; its openness to various and edgy gender, sexual and personal conditions; and its effort to maintain an authentic Christian Quaker identity while also being non-creedal and open to other theologies among its participants. This reviewer hopes these features can survive and spread, especially in the programmed and evangelical world, even if FFC doesn't. For that matter, if this combination is unique in their region, the elements are not unknown elsewhere. And maybe Daniels' work can bring encouragement to other similarly-inclined groups far from Oregon.

To maximize this potential, however, the text needs a thorough proofreading and rewrite. Publisher Wipf & Stock did Daniels no favors in their editing; if in fact they did any editing at all. Regrettably, a plethora of gaffes gets in the text's way throughout. As an editor-author I know we are now in the era where being sticklers about grammar and typos is increasingly obsolete, and my own performance is by no means flawless. One even gets the sense that it is bad form for an older Quaker writer to chide a younger one about this; so call me hidebound or whatever.

But truth requires saying that this text is internally defaced beyond any scholarly work I have seen in a long time. If the *Oxford Handbook of Quaker Studies,* from Oxford University Press, had typos on practically every page (which it did; see QT#24, http://quakertheology.org/Fager-Review-Oxford-Handbook-of-Quaker-Studies.html), Daniels' text has them in almost half the paragraphs. And not just typos: there are chronic grammar issues, such as frequent subject-verb disagreement, and jarring misspellings. The reader might pass by when John Bellers is rendered John "Bellars" once; but after the sixth occurence, attention must be paid.

The text is also highly repetitive; it could be cut by half or more, and be tighter, more reader-friendly and persuasive.

It would be better still if the revisions could include at least a brief survey of the movement's numerous predecessors. After all, while everything else about these latest New Quakers' future may still be uncertain, the one sure thing is that these are the greying ranks they'll soon be joining. If they're very lucky, the next batch may even remember them; but they better not count on it.

About the Contributors

Chuck Fager is Editor of *Quaker Theology*. His most recent book is *Selma 1965: The March That Changed The South. 50th Anniversary Edition.*

Douglas Gwyn is pastor of the Durham Friends Meeting in Durham, Maine. He has been a Quaker Studies teacher at both Pendle Hill and Woodbrooke in Britain. Among his books are *Apocalypse of the Word*, and *Seekers Found*.

Hugh Rock took up the study of theology after early retirement in 2007 and returned to study to gain an MSc in Social and Political Theory and a Postgraduate Diploma in theology from King's College London. His book *God Needs Salvation: A New Vision of God for the Twenty First Century,* (christian-alternative.com) takes up principles of Quaker theology for a universal future religion. He hosts the website socialtheism.org which aims to voice the religion in those lives that are by convention labelled, "not religious". Hugh is a new attender at Henley on Thames Meeting, Berkshire UK.

**Put *Quaker Theology* In Your Mailbox –
And your Meeting Library:**

A subscription to *Quaker Theology* will be a valuable addition to the reading matter of Friends meetings and schools. It will also help support our ongoing work of sustaining a progressive journal and forum for discussion and study. It's economical too.

Will you pass this form on to your Library Committee? Or better yet, make a gift of a subscription to your meeting?

Thank Thee!

Please enter a subscription to *Quaker Theology*

____1 year (two issues) $20

____2 years (four issues) $35

(Overseas subscribers: US$30 per year.)

NAME_____

ADDRESS:_____

_____Zip/Post Code_____

Send this form and payment to:

Quaker Theology
P.O. Box 3811
Durham NC 27702

Quaker Theology – There's Nothing Else Like It.

Made in the USA
Middletown, DE
24 March 2015